The Walter Lynwood Fleming
Lectures in Southern History
Louisiana State University

From
Rebellion
to
Revolution

From Rebellion to Revolution

Afro-American Slave Revolts in the Making of the Modern World

EUGENE D. GENOVESE

Louisiana State University Press
Baton Rouge and London

Designer: Albert Crochet
Typeface: VIP Garamond no. 3
Typesetter: G & S Typesetters, Inc.

Second Printing (September, 1981)

LIBRARY OF CONGRESS CATALOGING IN PUBLICATION DATA

Genovese, Eugene D   1930–
   From rebellion to revolution.

   (The Walter Lynwood Fleming lectures in southern
history, Louisiana State University)
   Bibliography: p.
   1.   Slavery in America.   2.   Slavery in the United
States—Insurrections, etc.   3.   Maroons.   I.   Title.
II.   Series: Walter Lynwood Fleming lectures in
southern history.
HT1048.G43   301.44'93'0973   79–17722
ISBN 0–8071–0586–4

Men must be caressed or annihilated, for they will revenge themselves for small injuries but cannot do so for great ones. The injury
that we do to a man must, therefore, be such that we need not fear
his vengeance.

Niccolò Machiavelli,
The Prince

A man may perish by the sword, yet no man draws the sword to
perish, but to live by it.

James Harrington,
A System of Politics

For Eric Hobsbawm
Our Main Man

Federico,
tú ves el mundo, las calles,
el vinagre,
las despedidas en las estaciones
cuando el humo levanta sus ruedas decisivas
hacia donde no hay nada sino algunas
separaciones, piedras, vías férreas.

Hay tantas gentes haciendo preguntas
por todas partes.
Hay el ciego sangriento, y el iracundo, y el
desanimando,
y el miserable, el árbol de las uñas,
el bandolero con la envidia a cuestas.

Así es la vida, Federico, aquí tienes
las cosas que te puede ofrecer mi amistad
de melancólico varón varonil.
Ya sabes por ti mismo muchas cosas,
y otras irás sabiendo lentamente.

Pablo Neruda

Contents

Preface

I

Enslavement in any form has figured as the antithesis of that individual autonomy considered the essence of freedom in modern societies. The revolt against slavery thus emerged as the basic assertion of human dignity and of humanity itself. The power of slavery as a cultural myth in modern societies derives from its antithetical relationship to the hegemonic ideology of bourgeois social relations of production. The dominant liberal and democratic strands of bourgeois ideology demand the responsibility of the individual for himself in the polity, the economy, the society. To be sure, working men and women have largely been excluded from the governance and benefits, but the justification for their exclusion has been compatible with the notion of propertied male individualism rather than in cynical or flagrant violation of it.

In bourgeois theory, freedom emerges as an absolute quality and right of the human being. Unlike some mystical or spiritual right that might be realized only in another life, bourgeois freedom is grounded in the solid here-and-now of absolute property. Those who do not possess external, material resources enjoy a minimal property in themselves, most notably in their labor-power. Marx might call wage-labor wage-slavery, but his metaphor draws its force from a general acceptance of an ideology that denies slavery as an acceptable social and personal condition.

Precapitalist societies did not readily raise movements of opposition to slavery, for they viewed social participation within one or another notion of society as a totality—normally, a hierarchically ordered community or household. Precapitalist societies have also tended to favor a more complex system of social participation. Less likely than capitalist societies to offer a single acceptable model of social being— the autonomous individual—they were more likely to justify slavery as a form of social being different from alternative forms in degree rather than kind. In this context, revolt against slavery generally took the form of simple revolt against unbearable exploitation or against the overstepping of traditional arrangements. Even the slaves perceived their revolts as external to society—as a withdrawal from society. For a long time, therefore, slave revolts had a restorationist or isolationist, rather than a revolutionary, content.

The objective social character of such early slave revolts should not obscure the deep experience of enslavement—of oppression and exploitation—that binds them to slave revolts in the modern world. Violent confrontation with injustice lay at the core of any revolt against slavery. But the goals of the revolts and the terms in which they were cast changed with the revolutionary changes in the social relations of production and the ideology of European and American society as a whole.

European conquerors introduced slavery into the Americas. The character of slavery bore the stamp of the historical development and aspirations of its progenitors. Never an independent mode of production or form of government, slavery in the Americas constituted a social formation and a particular set of social relations of production within a declining seigneurial ("feudal") and a rising capitalist mode of production, under the governance of the attendant political relations of property and authority.

The institutions of enslavement introduced by Europeans varied in their particulars from place to place throughout the colonies. The stage of historical development within the country of origin at the moment of initial colonization and of the institution of colonial government had a decisive impact upon the shape of colonial institutions, including the regional form of slavery. I have discussed the world-fashioning action of the master classes in *The World the Slaveholders Made*, in which I have sketched the historical context of modern slavery and, by extension, of the revolt against it. The initial impetus for colonization, whether that of a class, a segment of a class, or a government, frequently left a decisive imprint upon colonial institutions. The country of origin's form of government, as well as its religion, intersected with the level of development of the world market and the colony's actual or potential relationship to it in such a way as to favor a particular form of slavery. Frequently, market possibilities combined with scruples about, or impediments to, the enslavement of one's own people or of indigenous colonial peoples accounted for the systematic adoption of black slavery as the preferred form of labor.

Once a slave system had been inaugurated, however, it could be modified either by changing economic opportunities or by the perceived need of the masters to establish some form of social hegemony to mitigate or legitimate the brute economic exploitation. As I have argued at length in *Roll, Jordan, Roll*, the slaves never constituted a blank slate in this process. The successive waves of Africans brought with them as many commitments to and preconceptions of justice and legitimacy as their captors did. And they fought tenaciously, by all available means, including the ultimate confrontation of revolt, to enforce their own view of social relations. The slave societies that resulted from these continuing struggles bore distinctive features and embedded—even when they did not openly manifest—their own specific history of class confrontation and hard-won compromise.

These regional slave societies all took root and grew within an economic context determined by the prevailing European mode of production. And with due respect for the special cases of England, the Netherlands, and their respective colonies, that mode of production was, at the genesis of the American slave systems, seigneurial. The seigneurial mode of production that spawned the expansion cannot be equated with that of hey-day medieval seigneurialism. Internal crises had already permitted commercial capital and the absolute state to make significant inroads. In France, Spain, and Portugal, commercial capital nonetheless remained parasitic and fed off the prevailing seigneurial social relations of production, as even the most vigorous absolute state did. The dazzling achievements of the various monarchies never freed them from their symbiotic relationship with the seigneurial ruling classes. Nor could those ruling classes decisively free themselves from their ideologically and legally hedged relations with their own laboring classes without sacrificing the essence of their privileged position in their national community.

Just as colonization promised a multitude of economic advantages external to the precariously balanced national social system, so slavery appeared to offer, in one case after another, a means of rationalizing the social relations of production. But the various slaveholders, whatever their particular religious and cultural sensibilities, never intended that rationalization to impinge upon the traditional legitimization of their own status, nor upon their privileged access to property and authority. Rather, *grosso modo*, they expected their ownership and exploitation of slaves to buttress their position as seigneurs. If they could live with the distinct economic advantages of being modern *feudataires*, they rarely aspired to become capitalist entrepreneurs. And the vicissitudes of their continued symbiotic relationship with the denizens of commercial capital, who lubricated their operations and fed off their profits, confirms the persistent seigneurial context of their undertaking.

Even English colonization had its earliest roots in a precapitalist economic and social system. But the first great bourgeois revolution owed its origins to the same phenomena that produced the colonization and swiftly altered the larger legal and economic framework of its development. The great wave of slave imports into the Anglo-Saxon colonies occurred at almost the same moment as the Glorious Revolution, which confirmed the triumph of bourgeois individualism in the mother country. This transformation reinforced the ability of the Anglo-Saxon colonists to hold other men as absolute bourgeois property. To the extent that they sought to cast this naked exploitation as a viable social order, they turned to older seigneurial norms appropriate to relations between peasants and lords, rather than toward the barely emerging norms appropriate to free labor.

The history of slavery and of slave revolts in the Americas corresponds roughly to the transition from seigneurialism to capitalism. And like that protracted and portentous transition, slavery in the Americas cannot be reduced to any simple model. As a set of social relations of production embedded in a dominant mode of production, it must be apprehended by that nuanced vision which should inform any understanding of the historical role of commercial capital. For like commercial capital, with which it was so clearly associated, slavery in the Americas remained a rationalization of parasitism. Capable of extraordinary efficiency within a given conjuncture, it nonetheless represented a developmental dead end. Ideologically, it combined traditional and progressive elements in an uneasy and contradictory synthesis that inevitably conflicted with one or more elements of the emerging bourgeois ideology.

Nothing better testifies to the integral role of slavery in the transition from seigneurialism to capitalism—in ideological as well as socioeconomic terms—than the history of the slave revolts. Nor can any other social movement better illuminate the rich and contradictory process whereby the slaves fashioned their own history within the contours of the dominant modes of production. Throughout the seventeenth and most of the eighteenth century, the numerous slave revolts followed a generally restorationist course. The various slave populations with their discrete African and Afro-American cultures rose against the oppression of their European and white-creole masters. In so doing, they drew upon their own cultural identities and collective commitments to reject oppression and to advance alternative social norms. When their path did not lead to bloody defeat and heroic sacrifice of life, it led to a withdrawal from colonial society and to the establishment of maroon societies. This particularism, with its acceptance of social and political heterogeneity, might entail not only the re-creation of traditional communities but even the exploitation of other slaves. It also lent itself to deals with colonial governments or ruling classes that still accepted a hierarchically organized, particularist vision of social order. Thus, prior to the triumph of the capitalist mode of production and a cohesive bourgeois ideology, slaves could use the colonial world, at the margin, to defend their traditional conceptions of their own rights.

The conquest of state power by the representatives of the consolidating bourgeoisie in France decisively transformed the ideological and economic terrain. Nothing changed overnight, but the French Revolution provided the conditions in which a massive revolt in Saint-Domingue could become a revolution in its own right. The brilliance with which Toussaint L'Ouverture claimed for his enslaved brothers and sisters the rights of liberty and equality—of universal human dignity—that the French were claiming for themselves constituted a turning point in the history of slave revolts and, indeed, of the human spirit. Far from passively accepting the hegemony of the ruling class, Toussaint seized and appropriated that hegemony at a transitional moment. Henceforth, slaves increasingly aimed not at secession from the dominant society but at joining it on equal terms.

II

Two criticisms of the book's thesis may be anticipated since they have already been raised in private communications from colleagues and comrades. The first comes from the Right; the second from the Left.

First, I am not implying some ideological homogeneity, much less coordination, either before or after the French Revolution, nor the disappearance of restorationist revolts at any point in time. And I freely admit that the mechanics of ideological transmission remain obscure and await intensive research. I do insist that the black demand for the abolition of slavery as a social system was something new and epochmaking; and that it could not have emerged as a worldhistorical power before the rise of a bourgeois-democratic ideology which itself extended the revolutionary liberal commitment to absolute property. The slave revolts, like so much else, cannot be understood outside the context of a developing world history within which the politics, economics, and ideology of Europe, Africa, the Americas, and Asia as well, had become inseparable.

Second, I do not deny that the slave revolts foreshadowed the proletarian and anticolonial revolutions of the twentieth century. But in time and place their character was bourgeoisdemocratic. The argument for continuity with later anticapitalist movements may be sustained but only at a different level of analysis, and it does not contradict the primary thesis. For reasons beyond the scope of this book but familiar enough, the overwhelming mass of ex-slaves passed into the rural proletariat or into what Sidney Mintz has called "reconstituted peasantries" or into semi-proletarian, semi-serf social formations. In each case, the bourgeois-democratic revolutions were strangled early; in each case the radicalism of the revolts against slavery passed into anticolonial or anticapitalist movements, although this process must be evaluated with full attention to the conservatism of some of those reconstituted peasantries and to the long political subjugation of, say, the blacks in the southern United States.

C. L. R. James raised this question sharply in his early work, as W. E. B. Du Bois did in *Black Reconstruction*. And in different form it has engaged the attention of Sidney Mintz, José Luciano Franco, and David Brion Davis, among others. It is not surprising that these scholars, all of whom have been deeply influenced by Marxism, should insist on seeing the world whole and on stressing the political implications of their historical and anthropological investigations. The relationship of this book to that extraordinarily complex question would require another book to explore. But I have written nothing that denies the historical continuity of the slave revolts with later social movements—a continuity that does not justify reading the present back into the past.

Until the Age of Revolution the slave revolts did not challenge the world capitalist system within which slavery itself was embedded. Rather, they sought escape and autonomy— a local, precapitalist social restoration. When they did become revolutionary and raise the banner of abolition, they did so within the context of the bourgeois-democratic revolutionary wave, with bourgeois-democratic slogans and demands and with a commitment to bourgeois property relations. The transformation of that legacy by subsequent generations is another story.

III

Throughout history slaves have constituted the most oppressed but not generally the most revolutionary of social classes. Historians of the ancient world have commented less on the massive slave revolts of the Roman era than on their infrequency, and some have plausibly argued that the stronger revolutionary impulse came from the nonslave lower classes and strata whose less complete subjugation provided more favorable political, military, and psychological conditions. Accordingly, the legend of black docility in slavery appears the more ironic as well as the more ludicrous, for, so far as the evidence allows generalization, no enslaved people in world history rose in revolt so often or in such numbers or with so large a measure of success. The slaves of the Old South rose much less frequently, in fewer numbers, and less successfully than those of the Caribbean region and South America, but they too made vital contributions to the history of revolt.

This short book makes no attempt to recount the history of Afro-American slave revolts throughout the Western Hemisphere—a story that might require ten large volumes to tell in adequate detail. Rather, it proceeds topically and addresses two main problems: (1) the conditions in time and place favorable to slave revolt and guerrilla warfare, which help explain the infrequency and low intensity of revolts in the Old South relative to those elsewhere; and (2) the place of slave revolts and guerrilla warfare, including the southern, in the international political movements that were making the modern world during the aptly called Age of Revolution.

I have proceeded on the assumption that the extraordinary scholarship of recent years has finally laid to rest the myth of slave docility and quiescence. Thus, I do not discuss noninsurrectionary forms of resistance nor even such insurrectionary forms as the impressive shipboard revolts in the slave trade. These subjects, important in themselves, bear on the themes of this book, but their inclusion would only extend the text without essentially affecting the argument.

I have decided to risk the ire of my colleagues by omitting the several hundred footnotes that cluttered the first draft. There is little new information here—only an attempt to bring a point of view to bear on materials familiar to specialists and available in the books and articles cited in the bibliographical essay. I have not even cited the sources for the few quotations from plantation manuscripts, narrative slave accounts, and papers in the British Colonial Office, since they provide illustrations but not "proof" of anything. The bibliographic essay, although hardly comprehensive, may nonetheless seem excessive for so short a book; I hope, however, that it will prove useful to nonspecialists.

Those infected with the current rage for sociological order and "structural analysis" will, I fear, be disappointed with the lack of precision in my presentation of the "factors" that conditioned revolt and guerrilla war, and with my decision to follow a literary rather than a model-building course. Several sociologists, most notably Marion Kilson, Orlando Patterson, and Anthony Synnott, have undertaken such model-building and have enormously enriched our understanding while doing so. I have read their work with the utmost profit and admiration and wish to express my indebtedness to them. My own general views, independently formulated during the last two decades, more often than not accord with theirs on essential matters. I have not followed their course primarily because I sense a grave danger in overstructuring these historical materials. At bottom, I agree with Herbert Aptheker's blunt remark that the "cause" of slave revolt was slavery. And, as in all my books with the partial exception of the sometimes mechanistic *The Political Economy of Slavery*, I have tried to profit from Machiavelli's argument for the large claims of *fortuna*. No model can do more than heighten our understanding of the probabilities, for slaves anywhere and at any time might take up arms. Since these sociologists have pushed their methods about as far as they can safely go and since the work of Kilson and Patterson is well known, as I hope Synnott's will be when published, I have sought to seize the advantages of an alternative presentation.

Acknowledgments

My book *Roll, Jordan, Roll* (1974) contains a long list of colleagues who graciously criticized the manuscript. Since the earliest draft of this book was originally included in that manuscript, many of these colleagues offered criticisms, which I can here only acknowledge generally. A number of them, plus some others, also read later drafts and, among other services, saved me from embarrassing errors and challenged fuzzy thinking: David Brion Davis, Sanford Elwitt, Stanley L. Engerman, Eric Foner, Christopher Lasch, James W. Loewen, Ken Lawrence, August Meier, Sidney W. Mintz, Leslie Rout, William K. Scarborough, Stuart Schwartz, Joe Gray Taylor, Bennett Wall, C. Vann Woodward, and Mary Young.

Robert Paquette, in addition to offering valuable suggestions, did yeoman work in helping me to prepare the Bibliographical Essay. I am especially indebted to him for drawing my attention to some important Spanish American works, especially Cuban, that I had missed.

I owe a special debt to Edward Whiting Fox for his editorial and substantive criticism and, even more, for many, if not-quite-frequent-enough, discussions and debates about history. His extraordinary erudition, friendly skepticism toward my Marxism, and unerring eye for posturing and cant make our family gatherings all the more rewarding.

Elizabeth Fox-Genovese performed her customary wifely duty of forcing me to rethink and rewrite and of slipping in needed sentences, paragraphs, and even pages. And she made me finish a book I thought I never would.

This book grew out of the Fleming Lectures, delivered in the spring of 1973 at Louisiana State University. The splendid hospitality of the Department of History was what one comes to expect from southern colleagues. Let me add only that I consider the department's invitation to be as high a professional honor as I or any historian of the South could hope for, and I shall treasure the memory.

ONE

Slave Revolts in Hemispheric Perspective

The deceptively simple question "What was a slave revolt?" has one compelling answer: a struggle for freedom. But it has other answers that point toward an understanding of the special character of particular revolts and of the historical process within which the revolts occurred. Resistance of one or another type, visibility, and magnitude marked slavery elsewhere. But everywhere slaves who took the insurrectionary road had to display extraordinary heroism in the face of difficulties—extraordinary even by revolutionary standards. Nothing could be more naïve—or arrogant—than to ask why a Nat Turner did not appear on every plantation in the South, as if, from the comfort of our living rooms, we have a right to tell others, and retrospectively at that, when, how, and why to risk their lives and those of their loved ones. As the odds and circumstances become clearer, there is less difficulty in understanding the apparent infrequency of slave revolts throughout history and less difficulty in appreciating the extent of the rebels' courage and resourcefulness and the magnitude of their impact on world history.

The revolts of black slaves in the modern world had a special character and historical significance, for they occurred within a worldwide capitalist mode of production. Accordingly, they contributed toward the radical though still bourgeois movement for freedom, equality, and democracy, while they foreshadowed the movement against capitalism itself. That foreshadowing, however, necessarily remained an immanent tendency; it could not manifest itself as such in an epoch in which a socialist alternative had not yet matured. Hence, the revolts must be understood primarily as part of the most radical wing of the struggle for a democracy that had not yet lost its bourgeois moorings.

The slave systems of the New World arose from a conjuncture of international and regional developments, themselves generated primarily by the exigencies of the world market. But some systems, most notably the Iberian, had roots in seigneurial metropolises, whereas others, most notably the English, had roots in the world's most advanced bourgeois metropolis. Regionally, conditions varied enormously. Paradoxically, the English colonies of North America generated the slave system in which the master-slave relationship most profoundly affected regional history, for there the slaveholders most closely approximated a class-for-itself with considerable political power and autonomous aspirations. The English colonies in the Caribbean, in contrast, generated the slave system most thoroughly bourgeois and subservient to world capitalism. Having discussed these problems elsewhere,* I shall here restrict myself to the point most directly relevant to the revolts in the New World as a whole: Whatever else may be said of the revolts, they everywhere formed part of the political opposition to European capitalism's bloody conquest of the world and attendant subjugation of the colored peoples.

---

* *The World the Slaveholders Made: Two Essays: An Interpretation* (New York, 1969), Part One.

By the end of the eighteenth century, the historical content of the slave revolts shifted decisively from attempts to secure freedom from slavery to attempts to overthrow slavery as a social system. The great black revolution in Saint-Domingue marked the turning point. To understand this epoch-making shift, the revolts in the United States, or in any other country, must be viewed in a hemispheric, indeed world, context. I hope, however, that no one commits the mechanistic error of reading the argument to mean that no hints of the bourgeois-democratic character of the post-Haitian slave revolts appeared prior to the late 1790s or that no revolts of a primarily pre-Haitian character appeared afterwards. I hope, too, that no one interprets the argument for a decisive ideological shift to mean that it came clean, fully conscious, or without innumerable contradictions. A full history of the revolts would have to explore those problems in depth; here, we shall have to settle for a delineation of contours.

Many revolts began as more or less spontaneous acts of desperation against extreme severity, hunger, sudden withdrawal of privileges, or other local or immediate conditions. These sometimes but not often passed into warfare against particular injustices even as defined by the customary arrangements of slavery. Other revolts, as well as guerrilla wars waged by maroons (*i.e.*, groups of runaway slaves) aimed at withdrawing from slave society in an attempt to resurrect an archaic social order often perceived as traditionally African but invariably a distinct Afro-American creation. There appeared, especially during the late eighteenth and the nineteenth centuries, revolts aimed at overthrowing slavery as a social system—a magnificent object unknown to the slaves of the ancient world—and at winning for black peoples a place in the modern system of nation-states. The nineteenth-century revolts in the Old South formed part of this epoch-making transformation in the relations of class and race in the Western Hemisphere.

The most important slave revolts in the English-speaking North American states occurred in New York City in 1712; at Stono, South Carolina in 1739; in southern Louisiana in 1811; and in Southampton County, Virginia under Nat Turner in 1831. To them might be added the conspiracy at Point Coupee, Louisiana, in 1795, before the cession of the colony to the United States, and the conspiracies of Gabriel Prosser in Richmond, Virginia, in 1800 and of Denmark Vesey in Charleston, South Carolina in 1822. The brutally suppressed conspiracy of 1741 in New York City, however, seems largely to have been a figment of white hysteria, although some room for doubt remains. Other actions, realized and aborted, took place within narrow limits and engaged small numbers. Most states smashed plots, real and imagined, and periodically quaked with fear without suffering substantial revolts. The authorities may have suppressed evidence of some revolts, but they could hardly have done so successfully if they had had to contend with significant numbers or a large area.

The slaves of the Old South had a history radically different in certain essential respects from that of the slaves of the Caribbean islands and South America. The slave regime in the United States entered its great period of territorial, economic, and demographic expansion after the slave trade had closed; the prospect of windfall profits emerged at the very moment it became necessary to improve the material conditions of slave life in order to guarantee an adequate rate of reproduction. This conjuncture proved decisive to the flowering of paternalism and for the process within which the slaves increasingly were led to an accommodation with the regime, albeit a contradictory and violent accommodation.

Paternalism had taken root in Maryland and Virginia even before the closing of the slave trade had driven up slave prices and compelled the owners to concern themselves with the minimal welfare of their slaves. The eighteenth-century depression in the tobacco market squeezed the slaveholders, who increasingly found slave prices driven up by the more favorable conditions in the sugar market. Hence, economic conditions during the eighteenth century produced, prematurely as it were, an effect in the tobacco areas of a kind that would become general in the South once the international slave trade closed. The tobacco planters could make the psychological and political adjustment much more easily than the sugar planters of the islands could ever do, for they lived on their plantations in intimate contact with their slaves. As the proportion of creole slaves to African-born increased and the cultural distance between masters and slaves narrowed, the foundations of a regional paternalism grew progressively stronger. Yet, as the experience of the Brazilian Northeast shows, the ameliorative tendency in the paternalism of a resident slaveholding class, even one that inherited a seigneurial ethos from the Old World, could be offset by the economic pressures for increased exploitation generated by an open slave trade and the attendant low cost of labor.

The development of an organic master-slave relationship within the web of paternalism does not alone or even primarily account for the low incidence of slave revolts during the nineteenth century. Much less does it prove the slaves in-fantilized or docile. Without recourse to any such speculative psychologizing, it can be explained by a consideration of the specific conditions that encouraged slave revolt in the Carib-bean islands and Brazil but were largely lacking in the United States. The development of paternalism in the Old South—that is, the development of a sense of reciprocal rights and duties between masters and slaves—implied considerable living space within which the slaves could create stable fami-lies, develop a rich spiritual community, and attain a mea-sure of physical comfort. As they came to view revolt, under the specific conditions of life in the Old South, as suicidal, they centered their efforts on forms of resistance appropriate to their survival as a people even as slaves.

In no sense did that decision imply acceptance of slavery. The Spirituals and much other evidence attest to the slaves' deep longing for freedom. Nor did it guarantee peaceful rela-tions with their masters and with whites generally. Both violent and nonviolent resistance to injustice marked every day of the slave regime. And when, as in some noteworthy cases, slaves aboard ships in the domestic slave trade rebelled and steered for Haiti or for the protection of the British, they demonstrated that the appearance of favorable conditions and a genuine chance of success could trigger bold action. But, resistance and violence in daily affairs usually represented the settling of personal or local scores rather than a collective attempt to overthrow an overwhelming white power.

The religion the slaves fashioned for themselves fully re-vealed these contradictions. Led by their own black preachers and exhorters, the slaves did not simply imbibe white Chris-tianity. They blended it with their own folk religion, partly

6

African in origin, and thus created a message of love and mutual support, of their own worth as black people, and of their ultimate deliverance from bondage. Their Christianity served as a bulwark against the dehumanization inherent in slavery. But increasingly, black preachers understood, especially after the failure of Gabriel Prosser, Denmark Vesey, and Nat Turner, that revolt would be suicidal, and, therefore, with few important exceptions, they counseled a defensive strategy of survival. Thus, the social content of black religion became circumscribed by wider political realities, which it then reinforced. As the moral content of the religion emerged to justify accommodation and compromise as a properly Christian response, it simultaneously drew the teeth of political messianism and revolutionary millenialism. The development of black Christianity did not arise mechanically from the failure of slave revolts; nor can the failure of slave revolts be attributed to black Christianity.* Each arose within the totality of social relations and steadily reinforced the other.

Were the slaves in the United States unwilling or simply unable to rise in large numbers? The question ultimately lapses into absurdity. If a people, over a protracted period, finds the odds against insurrection not merely long but virtually certain, then it will choose not to try. To some extent this reaction represents decreasing self-confidence and increasing fear, but it also represents a conscious effort to develop an alternative strategy for survival.

The slaves of the Old South never gave up their expectation of deliverance and did not expect it to be handed to them without effort of their own. But the strategy for survival

* I am amazed that some critics have attributed such a view to my *Roll, Jordan, Roll* (New York, 1974). Nothing in the book supports so bizarre a reading.

7

a people, implicit in their magnificent religion and day-to-day resistance-in-submission to what could not be avoided, claimed its own price. The religiously grounded ideology of accommodation, understood as itself a vital form of resistance to dehumanization and to enslavement, acted as a powerful brake on the revolutionary impulse, to which it posed a realistic alternative.

The slaves' religion muted but by no means wholly repudiated the revolutionary message in the prophetic tradition. The strategy of accommodation counseled patience and realism but did not destroy the possibilities for revolutionary daring. The slaves' ideology steadily reduced the probability of revolt; it did not guarantee that a sudden main chance could not be seized. Thus, the slaveholders' constant fear of a people who rose rarely and in small numbers stemmed from a hard-headed ruling-class realism of their own.

General risings of thousands, such as those in Jamaica, Demerara, and Saint-Domingue, or even of hundreds such as those in many countries, remained a possibility, which, however slim, rendered the hopes of a Gabriel Prosser, a Denmark Vesey, or a Nat Turner rational. Turner did not succeed in raising the countryside *en masse*, but he might have, had he sustained his pilot effort even for a few weeks or escaped to forge a guerrilla base in the interior. Gabriel Prosser's supposed thousand followers probably never existed, but the legend itself may well have grown out of a plausible expectation.

The leaders of the conspiracy of 1822 in Charleston—"the most elaborate insurrectionary plot ever formed by American slaves," in the sober judgment of Thomas Wentworth Higginson—claimed to have enlisted thousands of slaves in city and country, and some historians have devoutly wished to believe them. But what should these tough rebels have said?

8

"Well, chaps, all we have is a cadre of a few dozen, if that many, but we know in our hearts that the masses will follow us." That message would hardly have sounded a certain trumpet to people who properly assessed the strength of the white apparatus. Vesey, an uncommonly able and sophisticated man, understood that the more people he had to confide in, the greater the danger of betrayal; and Gabriel Prosser before him and Nat Turner afterwards understood too. Initially, Vesey needed captains more than soldiers, for circumstances did not permit his training a large army. Charleston, a beautiful, charming—and well disciplined—city, did not present an ideal place to drill rebel troops. The captains would have to raise the army as they marched.

Vesey estimated, in effect, that the slaves, despite everything, would rise once confronted with evidence of success in a war in which they would have to choose sides. Nothing in the history of the Old South proves that estimate unsound —only painfully difficult to realize. Good sense, then, called for working with a few people who would be capable of quick large-scale recruiting once the war had begun. Their chances depended on their prestige among the slaves, on their prior effort to stir up support without saying too much or being too specific, and on the soundness of their evaluation of the popular temper.

And it depended on revolutionary terror.* The recruitment of large numbers could not proceed in the abstract. Slaves, long conditioned to submission and fearful of being slaughtered, had to be made to confront a new reality. Vesey

---

* Under no circumstances should my discussion of revolutionary terror be read as a defense of terrorism per se—for example, that of the Red Brigades and resurgent fascist *squadristi* in Italy. *Terror* and *terrorism* are emotionally charged words with many different meanings. Any evaluation must be historically specific. Accordingly, here I mean neither more nor less than what I say about given historical problems.

appealed to the words of Jesus: "He that is not with me is against me" (Luke, 11:23). He expected to force his people to choose not between revolution and safety but between revolutionary and counter-revolutionary violence. He reasonably concluded that the slaves, notwithstanding their fears, desired freedom and identified with each other rather than with the whites, and he expected to lead an army of thousands. But, first, he had to seize and secure Charleston with a Gideon's army, much as three hundred or so blacks came close to seizing Bahia in 1835, when they too reasonably expected to raise the countryside once they had secured their base.

Vesey's problem foreshadowed that of national-liberation armies during the twentieth century. How often did we hear during the Algerian War that the *Front de Libération Nationale* was killing more "innocent" Algerians than it was killing Frenchmen? How often today do we hear the same accusation leveled against the rebels in Zimbabwe (Rhodesia)? And probably it is true. But the accusation comes with ill grace from those whose proudest boast has been that they have succeeded in "pacifying" subject peoples—in breaking their spirit and convincing them that "the smart move" is to "work within the system." Indeed, this very evidence of pacification then appears in the work of apologists as evidence of contentment and imperialist beneficence: The people know how much better off they are and would live peacefully under our rule if only they were not tormented by outside agitators.

Since the system in question happens to be one of national humiliation and social oppression, it is pointless to berate some people for regarding those who accept such shameful conditions as traitors. Who does not know that the French could not have held Algeria long without the passive assent of thousands of "innocent" Algerians? Or that Smith's regime in Rhodesia would long ago have collapsed were it not for his black troops and politicians?

Those who do not readily blame the collaborators argue that accommodation follows from a realistic appraisal of the relationship of forces, not from moral degeneracy. Very well. But this defense reduces to the proposition that opposition to the oppressor ends in death. If so, revolutionaries who have not lost their senses must conclude that they will have no prospects until the cost of collaboration rises to the level of the cost of rebellion. For only then will people be free to choose sides on grounds of duty. And it serves no purpose to pretend that "innocent"—personally inoffensive and politically neutral—people should be spared. The oppressor needs nothing so much as political neutrality to do business as usual: It is his *sine qua non*. He who wills liberation in a context that does not permit peaceful change wills revolutionary terror. No slave revolt that hesitated to invoke terror had a chance.

Even a brief review of the general conditions that favored massive revolts and guerrilla warfare suggests the special difficulties which faced the slaves of the Old South. Were a list of those conditions presented without regard for the presumed importance of one relative to the other, it would suggest a higher probability of slave revolt where: (1) the master-slave relationship had developed in the context of absenteeism and depersonalization as well as greater cultural estrangement of whites and blacks; (2) economic distress and famine occurred; (3) slaveholding units approached the average size of one hundred to two hundred slaves, as in the sugar colonies, rather than twenty or so, as in the Old South; (4) the ruling class frequently split either in warfare between slaveholding countries or in bitter struggles within a particular slaveholding country; (5) blacks heavily outnumbered whites; (6) African-born slaves outnumbered those born into American slavery (creoles); (7) the social structure of the slaveholding regime permitted the emergence of an autonomous black leadership; and (8) the geographical, social, and political environment provided terrain and opportunity for the formation of colonies of runaway slaves strong enough to threaten the plantation regime. The list may be extended, refined, and subdivided, but taken together, these conditions spelled one: the military and political balance of power. Slave revolts might anywhere, anytime flare up in response to the central fact of enslavement; no particular provocation or condition was indispensable. But the probabilities for large-scale revolt rested heavily on some combination of these conditions.

Having glanced at the social context here and discussed it at length in *Roll, Jordan, Roll*, I shall, at the risk of too schematic a presentation, comment on some of the other conditions. Economic distress provoked many big slave revolts in the hemisphere, especially in the Caribbean, where war and inadequate local provisioning often resulted in desperate food shortages and outright starvation. Pronounced hunger, occasioned by years of drought and depression, triggered, for example, the massive rising on St. John in 1733; and in Cuba, writes H. H. S. Aimes, "There has always been a striking coincidence of servile revolts and unrest and the periods of economical depression and political crisis."

Countless agrarian and urban uprisings throughout the world have grown out of acute hunger and deprivation. Slaves, like other lower classes, normally stirred themselves to revolt slowly and with difficulty. The whip of hunger often rendered them desperate. Some of the greatest revolts, however, came during periods of material improvement, which stimulated expectations. And, although the governor of the Cape Verde Islands once estimated that almost four thousand slaves had died from the effects of drought and famine, no revolt ensued. Even starvation might not be enough.

A general depression in the United States did not have the same effect on the slaves that it did in the Caribbean islands, for a much higher level of self sufficiency provided some insurance against acute food shortages. Depression led weaker slaveholders to try to sell and lease slaves, whose resultant discontent must be taken into account, but even selling and leasing slackened during general economic depression as the demand for labor fell. The food supply remained the critical question. There is no evidence of large-scale or frequent diminution during 1820–1860, the period for which the firmest documentation exists, and little evidence for the eighteenth and early nineteenth centuries.

With or without economic depression, a large concentration of slaves facilitated the organization of revolt. Slaves in the Caribbean and in Brazil lived for the most part on great estates that averaged between one hundred and two hundred slaves. In Venezuela and Colombia the slave revolts occurred in areas of similar concentration or in the mining centers and cities. For example, the gold mining districts along the Cauca River suffered revolts as late as 1842–1843. In the United States half the slaves lived on farms, not plantations, and another quarter lived on plantations of fifty or less. Large units provided a favorable setting within which insurrectionary movements could mature. Cities and mining centers offered some of the same advantages to rebel slaves as did large plantations: Leadership could more easily develop; centers of autonomous culture could more easily emerge; and conditions favorable to personal movement existed. Richard C. Wade, in his attempt to make Denmark Vesey disappear, has argued that the conditions of urban life militated against insurrection. But in the Caribbean, Venezuela, and Brazil, not to mention New York City, urban revolts did occur despite social conditions very much like those of the cities of the Old South. Revolts occurred in both town and country; on the whole, urban centers, like great plantation districts, offered especially favorable conditions as well as special dangers.

The countries of the New World in which slave revolts occurred most frequently and with greatest intensity had a high ratio of blacks to whites and slave to free. In British Guiana slaves constituted 90 percent of the population and outnumbered whites by between twenty and thirty to one. Jamaica, Saint-Domingue, and much of the Caribbean had huge black majorities, often more than 80 percent, and even in Brazil, which had a large *mestiço* population, blacks heavily outnumbered whites from the early days of the slave regime. As Captain Stedman wrote after his experience in Surinam, "Every part of the world where domestic slavery is established, may be occasionally liable to insurrection and disquiet, more especially where the slaves constitute the majority of the inhabitants."

In the most important of slaveholding countries, the southern United States, blacks remained a minority except in restricted areas. They constituted a majority only in South Carolina and Mississippi, where their proportion ranged from 55 to 57 percent. The proportion of slaves in principal states in 1860 was: Louisiana, 47 percent; Alabama, 45 percent; Georgia, 44 percent; Virginia, 31 percent; Tennessee, 25 percent; Kentucky, 20 percent. The southern slaveholders read the history of the Caribbean correctly and moved to end the African slave trade. State governments periodically debated the significance of white-black ratios in order to reassure themselves against a new imbalance. In the 1830s, Dr. J. W. Monette of Mississippi offered the conventional wisdom of his class, which for once had some merit, when he noted that since blacks outnumbered whites only in two states the regime need not fear a general rising.

The slaves required a heavy numerical preponderance to offset the enormous military advantages concentrated in white hands. The slaves in Jamaica, Saint-Domingue, the Guianas, and Cuba, at decisive moments, could feel their strength; the slaves in the United States could not help feel their weakness. As Bennett Wall has emphasized, the constant westward movement inhibited, although it certainly did not prevent, the consolidation of those intimate ties which conspiracies thrive on. Suspect trouble-makers could be sold out of the area with little difficulty, and, in any case, a reshuffling of local personnel was constantly taking place. Wall has also emphasized another geographic influence: Southern slaves were not concentrated in large numbers except in the sugar and rice districts, and even there the plantations were sufficiently spread out and the police apparatus sufficiently strong to discourage attempts at collective resistance.

The slaves faced this white majority virtually unarmed. They did have access to axes and other crude weapons; those who worked in the sugar fields, for example, carried knives large enough to decapitate a man with one strong blow. During the eighteenth century Landon Carter of Virginia noted in passing that every slave in the tobacco fields carried a knife of some kind for his work. More slaves knew how to use firearms than the law allowed, for planters often gave trusted slaves permission to hunt with guns; and being trusted did not assure loyalty during a rising. Some slaves carried rifles while standing plantation guard, and others surreptitiously obtained access to guns and learned their use. A former slave interviewed for the Fisk University Slave Narrative Collection claimed: "Culled folks been had guns all their life. They kept them hid." In apparent agreement, Colonel Higginson thought that most of the former slaves who joined his regiment had had some experience with firearms. And recent archeological excavations of slave quarters provide new evidence.

The slaveholders had nevertheless not deceived themselves when they minimized the danger of revolt on grounds of insufficient arms. In any given area only a few slaves would have experience with firearms and even fewer with their tactical uses. Thus, John Brown wisely planned to distribute pikes rather than rifles to those slaves who might join him. As a leading Mississippian remarked during the 1830s, European peasants had much greater experience with firearms than southern slaves did, and yet they could usually be over-awed by disciplined military units.

Even with some guns, the slaves faced overwhelming odds. The whites who filled the interstices of the plantation districts, the up country, and the back country raised their sons to shoot. Sharpshooting and extraordinary feats with arms became elementary marks of manhood. The white population constituted one great militia—fully and even extravagantly armed, tough and resourceful, and capable of all the savagery that racism can instill. In South America, in contrast, mercenaries filled the militias and often did little more than they had to.

The southern militia and armed settlers had, moreover, a powerful reserve in the federal army, rarely summoned to put down slave revolts but psychologically invaluable to the bolstering of slaveholder spirits and the dampening of slave hopes. Masters and slaves both knew that formidable military garrisons stood ready to reinforce wavering slaveholder militias. Although the troops under Wade Hampton entered the slave rebellion of 1811 in Louisiana only after the militia had restored order, the firmness and promptness of their movement reassured the slaveholders for the future and could not have escaped the notice of the slaves. After the Vesey crisis, Charlestonians pointedly congratulated themselves on the assurances of federal support if needed. The federal response to Nat Turner and John Brown in Virginia underscored the point. With a white majority surrounding even the areas of black concentration, the slaveholders had a strong hand to begin with, but, in addition, they knew, and their slaves knew, that the armed might of the United States stood in ready reserve.

The Gabriel Prossers and Nat Turners of the South, like rebel leaders in countries with more favorable conditions, confronted other problems almost as formidable. However much solidarity and mutual support the slaves demonstrated, their circumstances left much room for informers, spies, and traitors. In any delicate situation one might be enough.

Thus, Colonel Higginson explained the infrequency of slave revolts in the South by noting that the blacks saw all the power in white hands. He added, "They had no knowledge, no money, no arms, no drill, no organization—above all no mutual confidence. It was the tradition among them that all insurrections were always betrayed by somebody." During the Nat Turner revolt some slaves even sided with their masters, as some slaves did during many of the revolts throughout the hemisphere. But every popular movement swarms with traitors, spies, cowards, and *agents-provocateurs*, so that dealing with them becomes the first test of resourcefulness for a rebel leadership. The context remains at issue. Inadequacy of preparation and execution—of organization—accounted for the failure of some of the most serious slave revolts in the Americas.

The enormous advantage of maroon leaders over slave revolt leaders rested here: Whereas with a little luck maroon leaders could maneuver, break off combat, survive defeats, and learn from mistakes, slave revolt leaders normally had to stake everything on a single stroke, prepared without prior experience among people who knew they would be risking their lives on a plunge into the unknown. Thus, when Charles L. Redmond advocated encouragement to slave revolt in 1858, Josiah Henson heatedly countered that he would do everything in his power to keep three or four thousand of his people from getting killed in a hopeless cause.

Cultural influences also shaped the military relationships. Throughout the hemisphere newly arrived Africans mounted the most dramatic insurrectionary thrusts. Creole slaves sometimes found themselves forced to side with their masters against rebellious Africans in Brazil and the Caribbean. The great revolution in Saint-Domingue was carried out by a slave population most of which, in the words of the rebel leaders, "do not know two words of French"; the Bahia risings of 1807–1835 had an unmistakable African base; and the overwhelming majority of the revolts in the Caribbean before 1800—perhaps all the important ones—were carried out by Africans who were, or claimed to be, Akan. The creoles made a vital contribution to the history of slave revolts, the content of which they transformed decisively; but, with minor qualifications, their moment did not come until the end of the eighteenth century.

The Africans who entered the Atlantic trade as slaves may have included some common "criminals" in their own countries, for the African chiefs used the trade to get rid of anti-social and disorderly elements. But they included many ordinary people labeled "criminals" in order to justify their sale and some political rebels who had participated in revolts and maroon activity while still in Africa. The Atlantic trade did sweep up common thugs and trouble-makers, but also heroic rebels against oppression with prior experience in the organization of militant resistance to despotic authority.

In the United States the slave trade closed on the eve of the great expansion of the slave regime, so that a creole slave force of unparalleled proportions arose during the nineteenth century. The trade to the British Caribbean closed about the same time, but emancipation itself followed after a quarter-century of political struggle in England and declining economic prospects in the colonies. Reflecting upon the greater incidence of slave revolt during the eighteenth century than during the nineteenth and on the part played by Africans, W. E. B. Du Bois wrote in *The Suppression of the African Slave-Trade*:

> The rough and brutal character of the time and place was partly responsible for this, but a more decisive reason lay in the fierce and turbulent character of the imported Negroes. The docility to which long years of bondage and strict discipline gave rise was absent, and insurrections and acts of violence were a frequent occurrence.

As the number and proportion of creole slaves increased in the United States, so did the regime's military power. By the turn of the century, slave revolts, difficult to mount under the best of conditions, attracted only an occasional zealot, for the oppressors stood united and in full command of growing military power. Slaveholders throughout the hemisphere, being neither politically inexperienced nor stupid, did not readily court disaster by dividing their ranks. Like Metternich, they calculated that if the great and well-born would vigilantly man their posts, the people would not dare rise or would be speedily crushed if they did. The aptitude of hardened reactionaries for logic has, however, usually outrun their aptitude for self-criticism and for empirical verification of their self-serving theories. As if that discrepancy were not sufficiently dangerous, they have also exhibited an irresistible tendency to underestimate the ability of their lower-class enemies to do anything except manifest a presumed penchant for mindless violence. The slaveholders understood perfectly well that their strength resided in their unity. But unity did not come easily when they resided in colonies presided over by warring European powers. The white Jamaican slaveholders might control their property-holding mulattoes, although that division along racial rather than class lines would eventually cost them dearly, but how were they to control the Spanish or the French?

The Caribbean region, almost from the first arrival of the Europeans, constituted one grand theater of recurring warfare, declared and undeclared. When the region enjoyed peace the slaveholders and their military forces happily helped each other to keep the slaves down. Without the arrival of French troops from Martinique, for example, the Danes probably would have lost St. John to their slaves in 1733. Yet, the landing of unwelcome French troops in Jamaica sixty years later provoked several slave risings. During the Maroon War of 1795 the British could rely on help from Spanish Cuba but had to lament the drain on their forces occasioned by war with France. In earlier days when Drake attacked Nombre de Dios in 1571 and humiliated Spain by sacking Santo Domingo in 1586, he had carefully prepared the way by forging alliances with local maroons. The Spanish also knew how to play the game. British officials in Jamaica sent messages to London in 1730–1731, warning that an expected Spanish invasion would have substantial and carefully prepared black help. The Spanish made Puerto Rico a sometime haven for escaped British slaves during the eighteenth century. During the 1730s the enmity between Spain and Britain provided favorable opportunities for the slaves in South Carolina, whom the Spanish invited to cross into Florida under assurances of freedom. The Spanish correctly assumed that self-emancipated black warriors would provide a formidable border army. The major slave revolt at Stono occurred in this context.

Repeatedly, the French incited the slaves of the British, who incited the slaves of the Spanish, who incited the slaves of the French. The slaves needed little incitement but welcomed evidence that they had powerful allies with whatever motives. In the early days of the revolution in Saint-Domingue, Toussaint deftly used the Spanish, French, and English to torment each other while he built his own army, ostensibly loyal to whichever European power had most to offer at the moment. At that, the slaveholders of Saint-Domingue invited disaster by creating a racial chasm between white and mulatto property holders and thereby weakening their alliance with the Girondist bourgeoisie at the moment the *montagnard* threat was rising against both. Toussaint learned quickly to maneuver for advantage and provided an almost too-good illustration of Marx's dictum that ruling classes unwittingly forge the weapons for their enemies below. Once made victims of divide and rule, the people can learn its uses. Toussaint made a brilliant pupil, but we should not shower him with too many compliments on this particular count: He had such good teachers.

Brazil offers another major example of the importance of ruling-class divisions in the history of slave revolt and maroon war. Palmares, the greatest of autonomous black communities, arose during the seventeenth-century struggle between the Dutch and Portuguese for control of the Northeast; it grew strong during the long period in which the Portuguese army had more important things to do. Brazil remained internally turbulent through the eighteenth century, and the slaves took advantage of white divisions. Most notably, the Portuguese had great difficulty in suppressing *quilombos* in Minas Gerais during the eighteenth century, when the blacks repeatedly took advantage of the struggle between the government and the settlers. The Portuguese attempts to sell monopoly rights and to levy confiscatory taxes provoked a harsh reaction and resulted in the Emboaba War of 1711 and subsequent armed clashes that played into the hands of rebellious blacks.

The series of revolts in Bahia during 1807–1835 took place against a background of bitter factional struggle within the ruling class, acute inflation and the disruption of foreign trade, considerable violence especially in the cities, and the frequent risings of disaffected army garrisons. The Napoleonic wars had brought the seat of the Portuguese empire to Brazil, and subsequent events produced political separation. Provincial separatists, supporters of one or another court party, not to mention those who rose against taxes and the metric system, provided a constant uproar in a country with less than the best of armies and with a large frontier to attract fugitive slaves. During the second half of the century the new abolitionist movement, the crisis generated by the humiliating war in Paraguay, and the struggle between rising and declining groups of bourgeois and landowners created a tumult favorable to slave desertions, resistance, and organized violence.

In contrast, the slaveholders of the United States confronted their slaves from a position of unusual strength. They had no metropolitan capital in Europe to answer to and shared power effectively in Washington. When faced with the threat of slave revolt during the early part of the nineteenth century they suppressed internal divisions and established a political consensus by eliminating the slavery issue and settling all other issues, many of which evoked strong passions, without violence or visible rupture of ruling-class solidarity. Southern slaves had much less reason than Caribbean or Brazilian slaves did to believe that they could take advantage of their enemy's internal divisions, although they too responded not merely to accurate political reports but to unfounded rumors as well.

False reports of political dissension among the whites spurred slave revolts as readily as true reports did. The slaves had their own means of getting news of distant developments. In 1733, William Matthew wrote to London that reports of the rising on St. John had reached Nevis via the French islands. In 1816, a resident of Kingston, Jamaica, warned Earl Bathurst that the reading of the Registry Bill in Commons would have dangerous repercussions. "My Lord," he pleaded, "the mere allusion to the question [of abolition] has gone far toward effecting our destruction and renewing the horrors of St. Domingo. Intelligence has reached us of an insurrection in Barbados." Were these gentlemen referring only to news that reached the whites? Hardly. As testimony on the Jamaican rising of 1831 made clear, the whites talked too much, and the slaves heard everything. On Tortola in 1790, Barbados in 1816, Jamaica in 1831, and elsewhere in other years, the slaves rose in the belief that London had abolished slavery and that their masters, with the connivance of local officials, were suppressing the decree. Similarly, in the sit-down strike in Buenos Aires in 1805, slaves took militant action in the belief that the government had freed them.

The slaves were displaying an attitude common among peoples, even the most rebellious, who had grown up in a world of class dependencies. The Russian serfs presented only the most famous example. As Michael Cherniavsky has written in *Tsar and People*:

> Thousands of peasants literally risked (and lost) their lives in order to appeal directly to the emperor against their oppressors, despite the law that forbade the serf to complain against his master. Hundreds of peasant uprisings took place during the thirty years of Nicholas I, for which the justification was the utter conviction of the peasants that their tsar had decreed their liberation and that his order was being disobeyed and suppressed by the gentry and the bureaucracy, that is, by the State.

This spur to insurrection appeared in the United States as well but not nearly so often during the nineteenth as during the eighteenth century. Even as the secession crisis burned hotter, especially after Lincoln's election, it had the radically different effect of raising the expectations of emancipation to come rather than of proclaiming an emancipation established and suppressed. Lewis Clark, an ex-slave who escaped to write his own narrative, even suggested that when the slaves in Kentucky had heard of the emancipation in the British West Indies, they became less militant because they considered their own emancipation a matter of time. In part the southern slaves simply may have had more accurate information, but the slaveholders' power over their region, so clearly manifest in every phase of political and military life, must have set firm limits to anything the slaves could believe about a superior power in a far-off place called Washington. The slaves of the Caribbean knew that London had the power to abolish slavery, especially after it abolished the slave trade, but the slaves of the Old South experienced little or no exterior power except that of their masters, whose consent was necessary even to abolish the African slave trade.

During the colonial period the slaves could seize upon evidence of internal and external division among the whites more readily than they could after the Revolution. In addition to trying to take advantage of British-Spanish antagonisms, they responded to political excitement within the colonies. The revolt in New York in 1712 occurred while the wounds from Leisler's Rebellion were still open and the whites deeply divided; and the cloudy conspiracy of 1741 occurred during the War of Jenkins' Ear. After Independence, political conditions became less favorable, but Gabriel Prosser took heart from the American conflict with France; Denmark Vesey effectively seized upon the implications of the Missouri debate and even spread the false story that Congress had declared emancipation but that the slaveholders were balking; and Nat Turner moved in an atmosphere charged at once with rumors among white and black alike of renewed war with Britain and with hard evidence of antislavery disaffection among the whites of western Virginia. The slaves always saw and heard more than they were supposed to, even though the slaveholders determined that there would be as little as possible to see and hear.

The white South suffered from internal divisions, the most dangerous of which pitted slaveholders against nonslaveholders. Recent research into the politics of the 1850s suggests deepening class antagonisms, which spurred proslavery extremists to push for secession as a way of disciplining the white lower classes. But there remains no doubt of the slaveholders' hegemony—that is, of their success in confining all struggles to issues other than that of property. In other words, although the struggles between slaveholders and non-slaveholders, not to mention those within each class, were growing sharper, they were not over slavery in any way that directly threatened slave property. To the contrary, the non-slaveholders of the Lower South and of most of the Upper South reiterated their support of the social system. The whites of all classes effectively closed ranks against the slaves after, if not before, the Nat Turner revolt. Had the South not seceded in 1861, the class antagonisms beneath the regional consensus might have exploded and created new opportunities for slave revolt. Indeed, fear of such developments played a discernible part in the decision to secede and try to secure the slave states against internal and external threat. But, whatever the might-have-beens, the slaves confronted a solid and overwhelming white majority until the end of the regime.

The magnitude of the task facing slaves who chose insurrection suggests the importance of leaders with considerable knowledge of political events in general; of the divisions among whites; of military prospects and exigencies; of terrain; of the psychology of their people; of ways to get arms and train fighters; of everything. Mechanics, craftsmen, preachers, drivers, even house slaves played a big role in the great slave revolts. Both rebel leaders and supreme accommodationists came from the same ranks, for they were men of wider experience than ordinary field hands and had talents they could turn in either direction.

Slave society in the Old South provided less room for the development of advanced strata than in the Caribbean islands and Brazil. Those strata did emerge and achieve noteworthy results in the South, but they did so within conditions that minimized the prospects for revolutionary success and thus maximized the pressures for nonrevolutionary forms of resistance and self-assertion. Craftsmen, drivers, and preachers provided the indispensable leadership in the southern revolts, but on fewer occasions than their counterparts in other countries, not because of lack of will but because of fewer promising possibilities. The privileged strata of oppressed peoples, then as now, respond to opposing pressures, as Frantz Fanon especially has stressed. Being most exposed to assimilation by the dominant culture and its superior technology, they are the least likely to equivocate on the political issues. That is, either they identify with their oppressors and seek individual advancement or they identify with their people and place their sophistication at the disposal of rebellion. They thus produce a high percentage of leaders and traitors. Individually, they play a central role on both sides; collectively, however, they do equivocate and attach themselves to one or the other.

Until the nineteenth century, and even then albeit with altered content, religion provided the ideological rallying point for revolt. In the Caribbean and in South America religious leaders—Obeahmen, Myalmen, Vodûn priests, Ñáñigos, Muslim teachers—led, inspired, or provided vital sanction for one revolt after another. In addition to the Bahian drama, Muslims led at least two revolts—in Saint-Domingue and in Surinam—despite the numerical insignificance of Muslims in those countries. There is, however, no reason to regard Islam, Obeah, Myalism, or Vodûn as intrinsically more revolutionary than various forms of Christianity.

The influence of Islam in the wave of risings in Bahia may

serve as an example. Throughout the Americas, Muslim slaves earned a reputation for being especially rebellious. The political-religious ideology they brought from West Africa ill-prepared them for enslavement to infidels, whose power they were expected to resist. West Africans could have absorbed Islamic doctrines only indirectly, for the masses continued to adhere to the older religions until well into the nineteenth century. The ruling strata, however, had both religious tradition and some knowledge of the specific teachings. In the New World they had the incitement and opportunity to forge an ideology of resistance. To do so effectively, however, they had to eschew Muslim purity and assimilate much of the religious thought and practice of the traditional African and emerging Afro-American religions. Thus, the literate Muslim leaders in Bahia accepted many practices considered fetishistic and pagan by strict Muslim reckoning. As their syncretism bound them closer to the urban blacks, free and slave, their ideological hegemony prepared them to assume the leadership of a firm and disciplined revolutionary effort.

The Hausa emerged as the decisive leaders of the early Bahian revolts. Muslim penetration of Hausa territory in Africa dated from the fourteenth century. Some towns embraced Islam during the fifteenth and by the seventeenth had established centers of Muslim learning. The great majority of the people, especially the rural cultivators, nevertheless, continued to adhere to their traditional religions until the Fulani conquest of the nineteenth century. The Hausa masses may not have been converted to Islam in Africa by 1807, when Zaria fell to the Fulani and the blacks rose in Bahia; but they had already been disciplined to follow a firm Muslim leadership, which in the New World successfully advanced Islam as a religion of resistance.

In Bahia an Afro-Brazilian Islam brought together African peoples. The Yoruba, who had resisted Hausa and Fulani encroachments in their motherland, turned up as Muslims in Brazil. Islam in Africa as in the Middle East arose fundamentally as an urban religion, and the Yoruba (Nagôs, as they were called in Brazil), preeminently an urban people in Africa, were concentrated in the city of Bahia (Salvador) in large numbers. Despite their rivalry with the Hausa in Africa, they cooperated with them in Brazil for reasons that, while not completely clear, probably included the combined psychological conditioning of their urban past and present and the attractiveness of Islam as an organizing force. As Trimingham writes, "Islam, being a universal religion, spreads the conception of the inhabitable world along with that of the universal God and establishes a link between peoples who formerly had little to prepare them to live harmoniously together." Indeed, the ability to unite peoples of different cultures and socioeconomic systems into a coherent civilization marked the political genius of Muhammed and of the classical Muslim state-builders.

Afro-Brazilian Muslims played a prominent part in the revolts that shook Bahia during the early nineteenth century: in 1807, 1809, 1813, and with special force in 1816, 1826, 1827, 1830, and most dangerously in 1835. Ewe (Gêges), Nupe (Tapas), and other slaves and free Negroes participated.

The exact contribution of Islam remains in dispute, although the thesis of a *jihad*, advanced by Raimondo Nina Rodrigues and others, appears questionable in the light of recent evidence. Some have seen the revolts as ethnic with a Muslim gloss; others as a class struggle in religious garb. A series of powerful revolts that brought together slaves and free Negroes, Muslims and non-Muslims, Hausa and Yoruba, resists simple categorization. Yet, Nina Rodrigues well argued that the Muslims had a firm political-military tradition and leadership; that they taught their followers to read the Koran in a city in which many slaveholders were illiterate; that they enforced impressive discipline; and that they forged alliances among previously estranged peoples. Thus, however much weight must be given to more general ethnic considerations, the ideological and organizational power of the Muslims proved indispensable. And if the revolt transcended class lines, as R. K. Kent has argued in his attack on the *jihad* thesis and other schematic readings, it nonetheless promised a substantial measure of liberation to the slaves of Bahia and thereby demonstrated an essential class as well as ethnic content.

The great Bahian revolt of several hundred slaves and free Negroes in 1835 revealed general conditions that provided the context for the revolts of the whole period. Despite British pressure and treaty obligations, Brazil continued to import Africans, whose number in Bahia increased steadily. Although these new slaves came from various areas, certain groups, notably the Hausa and Yoruba, clung together in large numbers. Many went to the city as skilled workers and craftsmen and established ties with free Negroes of similar background and together formed a coherent community with literate and sophisticated leaders. The surrounding plantations had long suffered desertions that fed the *quilombos* and kept the entire region in disorder; and the arrival of substantial numbers of West Africans with ethnic ties to the city created new possibilities for urban risings capable of setting the plantations ablaze.

The revolt of 1835 struck terror into the regime, as well it might, since it came close to success. Hundreds of blacks gave an excellent account of themselves and were defeated only with difficulty. Had the rebels planned more carefully or just had better luck, they might have realized their hopes of taking the city by virtual *coup d'état* and then raising the countryside. Bahia had come close to becoming another Haiti.

Where religious movements could take such non-Christian forms the slaves were being called to arms by a deep commitment that, by its very nature, divided master from slaves and black from white. It had to be immeasurably more difficult to win slaves to a purely revolutionary cause, the ideological and emotional content of which actually linked them to their masters on some levels while separating them on others. In the hands of a skillful anti-Christian leader the religious cry could be made to separate the slaves totally from the white community and thus transform every rising into a holy war against the infidel. When master and slave appealed to the same God, the same book, the same teachings, the task of the Nat Turners became much more difficult. It did not, however, as Turner himself demonstrated, become impossible, for Christianity has had its own revolutionary history. The difference came not with the abstract character of the Christian tradition but with the reduction of revolutionary potential inherent in the deeper separation of religion from class and especially ethnicity.

A final observation on the relatively unfavorable conditions facing slaves of the Old South concerns the maroons. The most impressive slave revolts in the hemisphere proceeded in alliance with maroons or took place in periods in which maroon activity was directly undermining the slave regime or inspiring the slaves by example. In Venezuela, for example, the Andresote revolt of 1732 occurred in the context of a widespread maroon war. The Caribbean revolts often had maroon connections, the most dramatic case being that of Saint-Domingue. For reasons explored in Chapter Two, maroon activity in the United States, while by no means trivial, could not spark general revolt as readily as it could elsewhere.

The size and frequency of the slave revolts in the British Caribbean may help to put those in the United States in perspective. The greatest slave revolts in the Western Hemisphere, except for the world-shaking revolution in Saint-Domingue, took place in Guiana and Jamaica. Guiana (the territories of Essequibo, Berbice, and Demerara) provided a theater of war between the British and the Dutch, who alternated control, and it offered an extensive hinterland for maroon colonies and guerrilla warfare. Like Jamaica, Guiana boasted a slave-free ratio of more than ten-to-one. Taken together, the territories averaged about one significant revolt, not to mention serious conspiracies, during every two years from 1731 to 1823—that is, from the revolt in Berbice in 1731 to the massive revolt in Demerara in 1823. The record is the more striking in view of the relative quiet of the years 1752–1762 during which a firm Dutch-Indian alliance kept the slaves and maroons in check. Berbice exploded, however, during the 1760s, with revolts in 1762, 1763–1764, and 1767.

The Great Rebellion of 1763–1764 under Cuffy, an ex-driver turned cooper, engaged, according to some estimates, half the slaves in the colony and was by any standard massive. The rebels were predominantly Africans; creoles joined late, apparently under some duress, and quit early. Cuffy attributed the origins of the revolt to the severity of treatment and tried unsuccessfully to negotiate peace. Although his aims cannot be wholly deciphered, they seem to have foreshadowed Toussaint L'Ouverture's dream of an autonomous black state allied to a major European power. The defeat of the slaves led, as usual, to widespread executions conducted with all the cruelty Europeans invariably attribute to nonwhite "savages."

Essequibo remained stable after the unsuccessful revolts of 1731 and 1741 and the aborted revolt of 1744, and the center of resistance shifted to Demerara in the late 1760s. The principal revolts occurred there during the 1770s: two in 1772; another in 1773; and two others in 1774–1775, which amounted virtually to full-scale civil war between the black slaves and maroons on one side and the whites and Indians on the other. Another serious revolt broke out in 1803, and twenty years later the colony went up in flames. The revolts of 1794–1795 took place against the radical backdrop of the French Revolution, the fall of the Netherlands and proclamation of the Batavian Republic, and the division of the white colonists themselves along political lines, with one party's raising the Tricolor and proclaiming the Rights of Man. Apparently, the slaves were supposed to be too stupid or too cowed to make that message their own.

In 1823 the slaves rose on the east coast of Demerara. Before the revolt ran its course thousands from at least thirty-seven plantations had taken part, two thousand in one major battle. The rebels demanded emancipation and, apparently with an eye on future labor conditions, a shorter work-week on the plantations. They believed that the "Good King" of England had freed them and that the planters were holding them illegally. Under the leadership of Jack Gladstone, a Christian cooper, and a group of drivers, craftsmen, and even house slaves, they attempted to prevail by nonviolent tactics suggestive of a general strike. Rather than kill the whites, they imprisoned them, executing only two who refused to lay down arms. The white captives subsequently testified to having been treated humanely. This moderation availed the blacks nothing: They were put down in blood. But the revolt stirred English opinion and strengthened the resolve of the emancipationist party to be done with the tyrannical regime in the colonies.

The revolts in Jamaica fall into two phases divided by the peace treaty of 1739 between the maroons and the British. The slaves had risen in 1669, 1672, 1673, twice in 1678, 1682, 1685, 1690, 1733, and 1734, with 150 participating in the revolt of 1685 and 300 to 400 in that of 1690. Once the maroons had won autonomy, however, they entered into an alliance with the British. Thereafter, the slaves could no longer find refuge in the interior, for the maroons would hunt them down and return them to the plantations or, worse, execute them on the spot. Increasingly, the slaves had to bid for the abolition of slavery as a system—bid, that is, not as particular groups for their own freedom but for a social revolution and the freedom of all. This tendency, however, did not mature until the interrelated revolutions in France and Saint-Domingue created a new system of international power and a more coherent revolutionary ideology.

The pacification of the maroons made revolt during the eighteenth century more difficult and less frequent, but not less intense: In 1760, St. Mary's Parish exploded in a revolt of at least 400 slaves, which triggered other revolts, one of which engaged about a thousand. The maroons helped the British crush "Tacky's Rebellion," but not before Jamaica had been shaken to its foundations by Akan slaves-turned-warriors, called to arms by obeahmen. This revolt, and those of 1765 and 1766 marked the beginning of the transition from rebellions aimed at restoring an African past to the movements to establish a revolutionary future.

In 1807 the slaves heard of the abolition of the slave trade and assumed that it also meant emancipation. Convinced that the planters were thwarting the king's will as well as their own, they rose. In 1815 about 250 Africans, primarily Ibos, without any creole support prepared to rise. They were crushed. In 1824, 1,200 slaves on five plantations rose. They too were crushed. By the 1820s the full force of the new world-wide revolutionary era and of the emancipation struggle in Britain was being felt. The great "Christmas Rising" of 1831, with 20,000 participants, followed the tense debates in London; embraced the creoles; prefigured a modern black Jamaican nationalism; and despite its defeat helped seal the fate of the slaveholding party. The revolt represented the culmination of a new stage, in which the slaves could look forward to independence in a world of modern nation-states. And its rhetoric was not lost on those battling for the Great

Reform Bill as a means of staving off deeper social convulsions at home. Mark the year 1831. The men of power in London, who found themselves pressed by the events in Jamaica to settle the slavery question once and for all had also to reflect on disturbing news from Virginia.

Guiana and Jamaica had many fierce revolts, but some colonies had none. Trinidad escaped, and Barbados, despite conspiracies and disorders, had only one major revolt and that not until 1816. The contrast holds no mysteries. The Spanish had used Trinidad as a commercial entrepot, not a plantation colony. When the British spread sugar cultivation during the nineteenth century, large plantations did emerge. But on the whole the system had more in common with that of the northern colonies of North America than with the plantation colonies. British power in the Caribbean had become overwhelming by the time of annexation, and the prospects for peaceful emancipation were steadily brightening. The slaves bided their time.

Barbados, however, presents a problem, for it had been the greatest of sugar islands during the seventeenth century and hardly enjoyed a reputation for humanity toward its slaves. Richard Dunn has probably offered the simplest and best explanation: The island was too small. The slaves had no interior into which to flee and sustain maroon colonies and guerrilla warfare, and they had no hopes of holding off the formidable British military and seapower. Any revolt, therefore, had to be an all-or-nothing act of desperation with every prospect for ending in disaster. And the proximity in which masters and slaves lived maximized the whites' chances of strangling conspiracies before they could mature. The revolt of 1816 broke out in the context of the movement to accelerate an emancipation believed imminent and, therefore, sustains the argument.

The revolts in Spanish and Portuguese America also help put those of the United States in perspective. Plantation slavery, in contradistinction to the use of slave labor in ways tangential to the main economy, did not flourish in Spanish America as it did elsewhere. The Spanish, with an enormous pool of Indian labor to exploit, imported Africans as a supplement. Nevertheless, even before the sugar boom of the nineteenth century transformed Cuba, plantation districts did exist within the Spanish colonies, notably on the coast of Venezuela, Colombia, and Central America, and important mining districts in Mexico and South America came to rely heavily on African slave labor. Not surprisingly, these plantation and mining districts, in which exploitation often reached extremes of brutality, became the centers of revolt and maroon warfare, although other areas suffered lesser shocks from time to time. As early as 1522 the slaves in Hispaniola rose in what was probably the first black slave revolt in the New World.

Black slaves in Mexico mounted significant revolts in 1546, 1570, 1608, and 1670. In 1537 the regime smashed an elaborate slave plot to kill the whites, impose a regime on the Indians and mestizos, and re-create a traditional "African" society. During the seventeenth century the conflict between the English and Spanish for control of the Mosquito Coast of Central America opened the way to autonomy for an Afro-Indian people ("Sambo-Mosquito") that had arisen there. These racially mixed people of color allied with the English, whose own weak settlement they protected in return for recognition and independence. Thus, the Spanish, who periodically faced trouble from black maroons, not to mention from insurgent slaves like those who shook the San Pedro mining district in 1548, found themselves unable to dislodge either their main European rival or their dangerous nonwhite local antagonists.

In Colombia the slaves destroyed the town of Santa Marta in 1530, and, after it was rebuilt, inflicted much damage again in 1550. The rebel *bozales* (African-born slaves) in the Colombian interior mining district rose in 1548 and killed twenty whites while taking 250 Indian hostages during their retreat to maroon bases. In addition to mounting small revolts, slaves, four thousand in number, paralyzed the Zaragoza area in the middle of the sixteenth century.

In Venezuela in 1552, King Miguel's force of about eight hundred rebels shut down important mines until the Spanish, with Indian support, crushed the revolt. The great revolt under Andresote in the Yuracuy Valley in the 1730s annihilated a Spanish force of three hundred before being defeated by one of fifteen hundred. The slaves at Coro, where there had been an earlier slave revolt in 1532, followed reports from revolutionary France and in 1789 rose with expectations of French help. This massive revolt also succumbed to Spanish power supplemented by Indian allies, but its scope may be inferred by the savage repression, which included 171 executions.

Among the suggestive features of the Venezuelan revolts were the concern expressed by Philip V of Spain in 1716 that renegade whites were joining the black maroon colonies and the widespread belief that by 1800 the total maroon strength in Venezuela had reached thirty thousand. Leslie Rout, in his analysis of the Spanish American slave revolts, notes that rebel slave leaders often were creoles, and he has plausibly suggested the importance of roots in the colonial experience to the formation of effective black military leadership. In any case, rebel slaves periodically plagued the colonial regime throughout its history, although during the nineteenth century black action increasingly merged with the struggles for national liberation and assumed a different political character.

Afro-Brazilian slaves also created an impressive history of armed struggle. Small, local revolts occurred frequently, and the first four decades of the nineteenth century in Bahia witnessed, in effect, a protracted revolutionary war. Certainly, insurrection-prone slaves in Brazil as everywhere else faced enormous military, political, and psychological difficulties and could not often realize their ambitions.

The attempt to minimize the record of slave revolt in Brazil presented with special force in Carl Degler's *Neither Black Nor White* rests on some extraordinary reasoning. In Brazil as in some other countries armed resistance of slaves took the form of maroon warfare much more readily than of direct insurrection. This distinction draws attention to a different set of military and political problems but hardly justifies the conclusion that the record of *quilombolo* struggle deserves no place in the history of slave revolt. Degler writes: "Generally, the *quilombo* neither attempted to overthrow the slave system nor made war on it." That is, the *quilombolos* fought defensively to preserve their autonomous regions rather than to attack the slave regime. This reading represents, at best, a partial and misleading truth. Its core idea—that the *quilombolos* did not aim at the overthrow of slavery as a social system—applies with equal force to all the great slave revolts from that of Spartacus to those of black Americans until the late eighteenth century. Thus, by logical extension all black risings before Toussaint L'Ouverture's and some after it, should not be classified as revolts.

The record shows impressive slave revolts, strictly defined, throughout Brazilian history, although that which strikes one as impressive may strike another as trivial. The question reduces to "impressive relative to what?" Relative to the slave revolts in the United States, the Brazilian record, which includes revolts by hundreds of slaves in Minas Gerais and Rio de Janeiro, not to mention the events in Bahia, stands up well enough, although it could of course be dismissed by anyone for whom anything less than Saint-Domingue or Demerara hardly deserves notice.

Taken as a continuum—as the insurgent record should be taken despite the necessity for analytical distinctions among different forms of armed struggle—the revolts, *quilombo* activity, and the participation of slaves in such wider regional and social revolutionary movements as the Balaiada justifies the conclusion, insisted upon especially by Marxist scholars, that Brazilian slaves wrote a heroic chapter in modern history, all numbers and relativity games notwithstanding. Black participation did not, by definition, constitute slave revolt, but, then, neither did the movement of American slaves into the Union Army. Here at issue, however, was the destruction of slavery as a social system by the absorption of the impulse to slave revolt, directly manifested much more often in Brazil than in the United States, into larger forms of struggle with better chances for success.

The principal revolts of the eighteenth century in New

York and Stono engaged modest numbers in comparison to those in the Caribbean or even Brazil, but they were big enough to strike terror into colonial America: thirty or forty slaves in New York and perhaps a hundred at Stono, with the ever-present possibility of attracting more if they had sustained themselves awhile longer.

They had an impact all the greater since the slaveholders knew of the formidable revolts in the Caribbean and took an international view of the matter, thereby displaying greater sophistication than most subsequent historians.

Both revolts broke out in the midst of noticeable divisions within white society. The aftermath of Leisler's Rebellion in New York had left the whites divided, although not necessarily as much as the slaves may have hoped. Possibly, the slaves had no great illusions on that score but expected that conflicts among the whites had weakened the political and military apparatus. At Stono conditions were even more favorable: The whites had their hands full with hostile Indians and with black maroons in Florida as well as South Carolina. The slaves knew—everyone knew—that Spain and England were preparing for war and that the Spanish were offering freedom to runaway slaves from the English colonies.

African-born slaves dominated both revolts and appealed to the religious sentiments of their brothers and sisters. The New York rebels espoused traditional African religion, as they understood it, and called for a war on the Christians in a manner suggestive of the early Caribbean Obeahmen and foreshadowing the call to arms of the Vodûn priests of Saint-Domingue. The religion of the rebels at Stono appears to have been more clearly syncretic: Angolan slaves with at least a formal adherence to Catholicism could put ideological distance between themselves and their masters and enter more easily into alliance with the Spanish, notwithstanding the small irony that the Spanish were themselves slaveholders. Mechanics, craftsmen, and other skilled and privileged slaves certainly led the revolt in New York and probably led the revolt at Stono.

The revolt in southern Louisiana in 1811, although the biggest in American history, remains obscure. Between 180 and 500 slaves—the lower estimate probably closer to the actual number—armed with axes and other weapons but with few firearms, struck toward New Orleans. The slaveholders, supported by a free Negro militia and reinforced by federal troops under Wade Hampton, smashed the revolt quickly. But the slaves' inexperience and lack of suitable weapons had not prevented them from manifesting a noteworthy degree of military organization; and as if that were not enough to make the slaveholders fearful of the future, the free Negroes' loyalty to the regime, never fully trusted anyway, was partially offset by the news that at least one of the rebel leaders, Charles Deslondes, was a free mulatto from Saint-Domingue.

As soon as the blacks' ranks had broken, the vengeful whites began an indiscriminate slaughter, although the rebels had killed only two or three whites and had largely restricted themselves to burning the plantations. The whites summarily killed sixty-six blacks and subsequently executed sixteen leaders. The executioners cut off their victims' heads, put them on spikes, and used them to decorate the road from New Orleans to Major Andre's plantation, where the revolt had begun. The "savages" had been beaten. Civilization had triumphed.

Because the Louisiana revolt had occurred on the frontier, it had less impact on the South than three others during the early part of the nineteenth century, although two of those never came to fruition. The aborted revolts of Gabriel Prosser in 1800 and Denmark Vesey in 1822, and the bloody revolt of Nat Turner in 1831, coming in the two great, long-evolving, supposedly stable slave states of Virginia and South Carolina, terrified the whole country. The Nat Turner revolt especially stood out as a "cataclysm" and a "fierce rebellion"—to invoke the language of Aptheker and Oates—for the primary reason that it drew a considerable amount of white blood, more in fact than the much bigger and harder fought revolt in Bahia in 1835.

The Nat Turner revolt had much in common with the Gabriel Prosser and Denmark Vesey conspiracies. In each the leader had learned to read and write and had special talents and privileges. Gabriel Prosser was a blacksmith whose militant politico-religious temperament placed him in a long line of artisan and skilled-slave revolutionaries. Nat Turner, a jack-of-all-trades slave who basically worked as a field hand, was an exhorter. If Turner did not emerge as the skilled mechanic or foreman he has often been called, he had nonetheless had ample preparation for advanced work and could only have been embittered by the lack of opportunity. His parents and their friends had perceived him as a remarkable child with special religious powers and had predicted a great future for him as a free man. Vesey had bought his own freedom after winning a lottery: curiously, the year was 1800—the year of Gabriel's rebellion and of Nat Turner's birth. As a slave, born either in the Caribbean or in Africa, he had worked as a seaman and visited many countries, including

44

Haiti. He spoke several languages and read the political press. Vesey's first-rate group of lieutenants included the celebrated Peter Poyas, a ship's carpenter, as well as a slave foreman, house servants, and skilled craftsmen.

Each revolt took root amidst bitter antagonisms among the whites. The undeclared war with France led Gabriel Prosser to expect all-out war and French help. And, however much the Federalists and Republicans fought each other within a consensus, the inflammatory rhetoric and the appeals to and denunciations of French revolutionary ideology made a deep impression on the slaves, who may well have thought that they saw a white nation on the verge of civil war. Vesey and his followers eagerly followed the Missouri debate—that "firebell in the night," as Jefferson called it. Whatever interpretation the slaves put on the debate, they had firm evidence that antislavery sentiment was rising and that the slaveholders were being thrown on the defensive. Their reading was strategically sound, however much they may have misjudged the pace of events. And at that, they may merely have assumed that the political split was weakening the slaveholders to some extent. Nat Turner made his move after a tense constitutional convention in Virginia which embittered the antislavery western counties, displayed public charges of slaveholder tyranny over the state, and generated demands for abolition, albeit with colonization.

Each of these outstanding rebel leaders blended religious appeals to the slaves with the accents of the Declaration of Independence and the Rights of Man. Each projected an interpretation of Christianity that stressed the God-given right to freedom as the fundamental doctrine of obligation underlying a political vision that itself reflected the new ideologies

45

of the Age of Revolution. And each had to confront the African presence among his people. Gabriel Prosser, despite warnings from within his own camp, stressed Christian and secular appeals and, to his cost, slighted the folk religion of the country slaves, who retained stronger links to their African past. Nat Turner emerged as a messianic Christian prophet and skillfully spoke a language drawn from the radical books of the Bible and the revolutionary tradition of America. Yet, sober scholars have seen in his Christianity, notwithstanding his stated contempt for "conjuring," a strong African influence of which he may not have been aware.

Between the two revolts in Virginia Denmark Vesey had worked out the most subtle and sophisticated appeal. His movement boldly spoke both in radical Christian and traditional African—or what purported to be traditional African—terms. Vesey appealed to the Bible, much as Prosser had done and Turner would do, but he also relied on Jack Pritchard ("Gullah Jack"), an Angolan, to reach slaves who had not yet been converted to Christianity or whose conversion had been superficial. Pritchard, like many other leaders of the revolt, had been a member of the African Methodist Episcopal Church, which the authorities in Charleston had closed down as subversive; indeed, he reportedly had wanted to strike immediately after the repression, which had enraged him and the black community generally. In combining Christian and African appeals Vesey and his followers did not play a double game: They varied the accents of a black folk religion that was combining many sources and working itself out as a distinct Afro-American religious experience.

The appeal to African elements in the slaves' religion served a special function in bolstering morale among those who faced grim odds. The use of charms by the rebels in Charleston, as by slave rebels throughout the Americas, will illustrate. In many revolts slaves went into battle with charms that ostensibly protected them from the white man's bullets. The Reverend C. C. Jones of Georgia, in his *Religious Instruction of the Negroes* (p. 128), expressed particular uneasiness at the appearance of such notions among southern slaves. Well he might have, for they have appeared among insurrectionary peasants and the poor in Europe as well as in Africa, Melanesia, and the colonial world generally. This recurring use of charms has proven a powerful antidote to the normal fears among fresh recruits. However "superstitious," those who have gone into battle under this protection have usually had their reasons; they have been able to see their comrades fall, charms or no charms. The Reverend Mr. Jones wisely refused to take comfort in the taunts of the judge who sentenced Gullah Jack to death:

> Jack Pritchard . . . you represented yourself as invulnerable; that you could neither be taken nor destroyed, and that all who fought under your banner would be invincible. . . . Your boasted charms have not preserved yourself and of course could not protect others.

Religiously inspired rebels could always attribute the inevitable casualties to the victims' bad faith or failure to observe proper ritual or even to the prospect of reincarnation in Africa. They needed something to stiffen their resolve in the face of overwhelming odds, and their religious leaders pro-

vided as good a spur as was available. As Eric Hobsbawm remarks, "And, alas, the poor and the weak know that their
champions and defenders are not really invulnerable. They
may always rise again—but they will also be defeated and
killed." The promise of invulnerability, he adds in his book
Bandits, "offers in mythological form what every such rebel
knows he desperately needs—luck."

Slave revolt leaders in the South had much less to fall back
upon during the nineteenth century than their forerunners
during the eighteenth or their counterparts elsewhere in the
Americas. They were influenced by conjuring but were normally skeptical of its extreme and politically dangerous
forms. And they lived too close to their masters to deceive
themselves. As one rebel slave recruit in Missouri explained,
"I've seen Marse Newton and Marse John Ramsey shoot too
often to believe they can't kill a nigger."

The strategic aims of the revolts remain debatable, apart
from the straightforward goal of securing the freedom of
those in rebellion and of as many other slaves as possible.
Gabriel Prosser sought to seize Richmond—a realistic objective in view of its indifferent defenses—and to inflict enough
blows on the whites to bring them to unspecified terms. Possibly, the rebels would have tried to win recognition for an
enclave state; possibly, they sought freedom within existing
political arrangements; probably, they were waiting to seize
any opportunities that emerged. Vesey apparently tried to
keep several options open. Had he taken Charleston and secured its hinterland he might have set up an independent
republic, although he undoubtedly knew the odds against
holding out. He seems to have expected to sail to Haiti with
as many blacks as survived the early engagements. Turner's

objectives remain obscure. He may have thought along lines similar to those of Gabriel Prosser or may have expected to form a large maroon colony in the Dismal Swamp. Of all the major plots and revolts his displayed the least evidence of careful planning, preparation, and foresight. Yet, this very weakness may have given it a strength denied to Prosser and Vesey, for it was less exposed to betrayal.

Whatever the reliance on archaic ideological forms, the nineteenth-century revolts in the United States reflected the world as it was emerging in the era of the great revolution in Saint-Domingue and the revolutionary struggles in Europe and America. Their restorationist appearance—the possibility that each would have ended as a maroon enclave—represented primarily the impingement of military reality. Vesey looked to Haiti as a model and for inspiration as well as for material support. His speech to his followers combined the language of the Age of Revolution, as manifested in the Declaration of Independence and the Constitution, with the biblical language of the God of Wrath. Nat Turner, a messianic exhorter, also spoke in the accents of the Declaration of Independence and the Rights of Man. Nat Turner, whatever else he might have been, was a Virginian.

In general, then, the slaves of the United States faced a highly unfavorable relationship of forces, which shifted them away from revolt and toward other forms of resistance. The slaves had much better opportunities to revolt during the eighteenth than the nineteenth century; in general, their position steadily deteriorated over time until revolt became virtually suicidal. But even during the eighteenth century they never had opportunities as promising as the slaves of other countries had. By the time of Gabriel Prosser, Denmark Vesey, and Nat Turner only the most heroic souls, even as measured by the highest standards of revolutionary self-sacrifice, could contemplate such a course; and their prospects for raising the masses grew steadily dimmer despite the popular commitment to freedom. The wonder, then, is not that the United States had fewer and smaller slave revolts than some other countries did, but that they had any at all. That they did, in whatever proportions, demonstrated to the world the impossibility of crushing completely the slaves' rebellious spirit.

TWO

Black Maroons in War and Peace

The slaveholders of the New World faced military challenge not only from slaves in open revolt but also from those who fled the plantations, grouped themselves in runaway communities, and waged guerrilla warfare. These maroons (*cimarrones*, *marrons*, *quilombolos*) plagued every slave society in which mountains, swamps, or other terrain provided a hinterland into which slaves could flee. Some maroon communities became powerful enough to force the European powers into formal peace treaties designed to pacify the interior while recognizing the freedom and autonomy of the rebels. Jamaica and Surinam provided the most famous of these cases, which had counterparts in Mexico, Venezuela, and elsewhere. The Portuguese, as early as the seventeenth century, had unsuccessfully offered terms to the great *quilombo* of Palmares, and even the haughty French came to terms with several thousand maroons near the Spanish border of Saint-Domingue. The terms of the various treaties usually granted the maroons freedom and autonomy in return for a pledge of allegiance to the colonial regime, including the duty to return new runaways and to defend the public order—that is, to suppress slave rebellions. The Catholic countries also required adherence to the Church. Relations between maroons

51

and slaves after promulgation of such treaties became maddeningly ambiguous.

Most maroon communities did not have an opportunity to come to terms with the colonial regimes. They remained small units of tens or hundreds, sometimes in loose alliance but sometimes culturally and politically hostile to each other. So long as they remained outside the established colonial order they sympathized with the fate of those still enslaved, for their own guerrilla activities required intelligence and supplies from plantation informers and supporters. Everywhere in the hemisphere maroons at particular times and in particular places provoked desertions and slave revolts; they fought and often defeated the troops sent against them. Whatever their relations with the slaves, their success in defeating white military expeditions said more to the plantation slaves about the fighting quality of black people than any abolitionist pamphlet ever could.

Although varying greatly in time and place, the maroon redoubts in various countries had some common features. Especially when maroons secured periods of peace by compelling the whites to agree to a *modus vivendi*, they built agricultural communities that echoed Africa while developing as original Afro-American formations. Typically, the communities relied on horticulture and raised such crops as yams, sweet potatoes, bananas, plantains, squash, and beans, although they might also add cotton, sugarcane, and especially tobacco for their own use. They rarely if ever achieved self-sufficiency in manufactures and had to depend on others for cloth, implements, and, above all, guns.

When at peace with the whites and sometimes even when at war, these maroon colonies established trade relations with nearby planters and townspeople. Trade relations with the Europeans and the absorption of occasional white adventurers into the community provided some check to the thoroughgoing Africanization. Yet, on the whole these communities came closest of all New World black communities to recapitulating Africa, notwithstanding their remaining essentially American—*i.e.*, new cultural formations. Indeed, they seem to have preserved some features of African culture that were disappearing in Africa itself. But, as Gilberto Freyre argues for Brazil, they also spread European language, religion, and mores, however reshaped, among the Indians of the interior and thereby served as agents of Western cultural expansion.

Family and social life in general recalled African kinship patterns, and political leadership centered in religiously sanctioned "kingships." The maroons imposed strict quasimilitary discipline and inflicted severe punishments for violations of norms and challenges to authority. Much of the rivalry between competing maroon groups in Jamaica, the Guianas, and elsewhere, which sometimes flared into warfare, originated in the attempt of a leader of one maroon community to impose his will on others.

In different ways and in varying degrees, the maroon communities aimed at restoring a lost African world while incorporating features of Euro-American civilization and specifically plantation culture. The culture that arose on these foundations combined African, European, Amerindian, and slave-quarter elements into new and varied complexes. The Jamaican and Surinam maroons reworked their African inheritance by assimilating useful elements of their American experience; simultaneously, they filtered their American acquisitions through an African prism. African-born slaves, rather than creoles, sparked the establishment of maroon communities, and the societies they built reflected their origins. Creoles, however, sometimes became maroon leaders in numbers disproportionate to their place in either the maroon or general slave population. And, as Barbara Kopytoff has stressed, increasingly the big maroon communities fell under the leadership of their own creoles—of those born as maroons. The peculiar military and diplomatic problems facing maroons favored the rise of leaders with extensive knowledge of the country and experience in dealing with the authorities. The creoles, however, provided fewer maroons than the Africans did in part because they had advantages of language and familiarity with terrain and could fly to the towns and cities and blend into the free Negro population. Thus, the African predominance among the maroons does not indict the creoles for lack of militancy but, rather, delineates different paths of struggle. But since maroon communities strongly reflected the culture of transplanted Africans, they often presented the creoles with an unsympathetic, strange, and culturally threatening power.

During the eighteenth century the relationship of the maroons to slave revolts and the more general relationship of maroons to slaves became strained. In their formative periods the maroon communities, often fighting for survival, cultivated close relations with those remaining in slavery, relied on them for support, and encouraged them to desert and rebel. Even then, the maroons sometimes alienated the slaves by seizing their women and supplies. In time, two circumstances deepened the antagonism: The colonial powers sometimes offered favorable peace treaties to the maroons in return for capturing runaways and crushing slave revolts; and during the nineteenth century, as creole slaves increased relative to "salt water" slaves, the cultural gap between maroons and slaves widened and generated sharp hostilities and even hatreds. If the maroons sometimes let their treaty obligations to capture runaways slip altogether or met them indifferently, at other times they treated dissident slaves brutally. The record of the Jamaican maroons, although contradictory, displayed a well-known African respect for treaty obligations and word of honor. When they said they would assist the whites against the slaves, they meant to keep their word. Even after the defeat of the rebels during the most famous of the maroon wars in the 1790s, when the British cynically broke their promise not to expel those who surrendered, the maroons, after a brief stay in Nova Scotia, arrived as disgruntled exiles in Sierra Leone in time to put down a rebellion. Those who remained in Jamaica played an important role in crushing the Morant Bay rising of 1865.

During the revolution in Saint-Domingue the maroons sometimes sided with the whites against Toussaint's efforts to compel obedience to his authority. They greeted Napoleon's army, which came to restore slavery, as allies and later gave some support to their old archenemies, the mulattoes, against the blacks. Their course makes no sense except on the simple premise that, above all, they wished to protect their own autonomy against any centralizing power, white or black, reactionary or revolutionary.

Evidence of collaboration with whites notwithstanding, the formation of maroon communities generally had a destructive impact on slavery and provided a spur to slave disaffection, desertion, and rebellion. In Surinam, Venezuela, Jamaica, and elsewhere, maroons inspired slaves to challenge white authority and to rebel. When as often happened, the maroons were waging war against the regime, if only because it would not come to terms until being convinced it could not win, they consciously sought allies and reinforcements from among the plantation slaves. In 1733 the British received information that even their ostensibly loyal black troops were conspiring to aid the maroons. The authorities understood that unchecked maroons presented a constant temptation to the slaves to rise in revolt or to desert *en masse*.

Of special significance, maroons sometimes delivered hard blows against the whites in retaliation for particularly brutal treatment of slaves. In Surinam, for example, during the peace negotiations of 1757 a rebel leader rebuked the governor's emissary and asked how the Europeans could claim to be civilized and yet treat their slaves so cruelly. He then offered some advice, which tells us much about the ambiguities of maroon ideology. As Captain Stedman recounts his speech:

> We desire you to tell the governor and your court that in case they want to raise no new gangs of rebels, they ought to take care that the planters keep a more watchful eye over their own property, and do not trust them so frequently to the hands of drunken managers and overseers, who . . . are the ruin of the colony and wilfully drive to the woods such numbers of stout, active people, who by their sweat earn your subsistence, without whose hands your colony must drop to nothing, and to whom at last, in this disgraceful manner, you are glad to come and sue for friendship.

The maroon's concern for the welfare of the slaves, as reflected in this remarkable speech, revealed a willingness to leave slavery itself intact. Thus, the outstanding rebel leader, Baron, released a captured white army officer who had recently arrived in Surinam and undoubtedly expected execution: "Go away, for you have not been long enough in the colony to have been guilty of mistreating slaves." Another rebel chief, Araby, offered to send his son to Europe for a Dutch education if peace terms could be arranged, and a year later the rebels received the Dutch peace commissioners with a display of aristocratic hospitality.

Maroons, whether in Palmares, Surinam, or Jamaica, themselves often enslaved captives, including those already enslaved by the whites. They seem to have practiced a mild, familial slavery reminiscent of the kind ostensibly practiced in Africa. But those historians who speak of African slavery —or more precisely, of the indigenous forms of bondage called slavery by the Europeans—do not appear to have consulted the slaves, who may have perceived matters differently. No matter how mild the day-to-day existence of slaves in Africa, the threat of ritual execution hung heavily over many. In the maroon communities slaves do appear to have had an easier time, but without their own testimony we can hardly be certain. What remains certain is that many maroon communities did try to influence the white slaveholders to treat their slaves more humanely. The maroons' course thus simultaneously supported the efforts of the slaves to improve their condition and yet accepted the moral and judicial pretensions of the white slaveholders. Their course necessarily inhibited the development of an abolitionist—a revolutionary—ideology while the very existence of the maroon communities was sending revolutionary shock waves through the slave quarters.

From the early days of their conquest of the New World all the European powers applied the policy of "divide and rule."

Cortes, for example, wrote frankly about his reliance on the support of Indians who had suffered oppression at the hands of the Aztecs and were waiting for a chance to rise. Thereafter, the Europeans did their best to exacerbate tribal hatreds among Amerindians and later Africans, to foment hostility between Indians and Africans, and to set blacks against coloreds, creoles against Africans, and maroons against slaves. The policy produced generally positive effects for the Europeans in part because it had firm roots in traditional hostilities and even new ones that required only little encouragement from outsiders in order to burst into violence. Although imperialists of all ages have mastered the art of turning peoples' ethnic hatreds to advantage, it does them too much honor to accuse them of inventing those hatreds. They have rarely had such power. The Dutch, for example, would have had an even rougher time in Surinam had not one group of maroons adopted an offensive policy toward other groups and driven them into an alliance with the regime.

Indians and black slaves or maroons sometimes supported each other against the whites. The Indians might welcome black runaways or even negotiate a military alliance. Cooperation appeared everywhere, but so did hostility. Amerindians provided the decisive troops against black maroon colonies and slave revolts in Surinam, Brazil, Colombia, Jamaica, and elsewhere, and black troops helped to crush various Indian revolts. Some Indians at war with Europeans stole black slaves for their own use and thereby further complicated Afro-Indian relations. The Island-Carib, for example, conducted heavy slave raids against the British islands in the Caribbean during the seventeenth century, somtimes alone and sometimes in alliance with the French. This record of antagonism does not negate Roger Bastide's argument that, for the long run, Afro-Indian contacts shaped a wide-ranging syncretization and the rise of Afro-Indian communities.

Throughout the New World free Negroes and even loyal slaves periodically helped to crush slave revolts and maroon bastions. In Africa black troops provided an indispensable supplement to white in the coastal slave depots, and in the Caribbean, in particular, the loyalty of some slaves proved adequate to frustrate the militancy of others. The extensive report from Surinam by Captain Stedman sheds light on the more general use of loyal slaves against rebels and might, with only a shift in details, have come from Brazil or other countries. After having come to terms with two groups of maroons, the Dutch continued their brutal treatment of the slaves and provoked a new rebellion in 1772. A majority of the planters fled to Paramaribo in panic while the authorities made the desperate decision to form units of manumitted slaves to send against the rebels.

The black loyalists astonished the whites by their conduct under fire and, in Captain Stedman's words, "performed wonders." These three hundred or so blacks saved the day for the European slaveholders until Dutch troops could arrive from Europe, for the local colonial troops had proved inadequate. The authorities had picked their slave troops carefully from among especially strong volunteers with no record of recalcitrance. Owners received full payment in compensation. The Rangers, as the blacks came to be called, staked out an "implacable enmity against the rebels" and checked their advance with great ferocity. The rebels returned the hatred: They sometimes spared white prisoners of war but summarily executed all Rangers.

Captain Stedman explains the Rangers' tenacity as a consequence of their desire to earn freedom. He also observes that, once having made the decision to fight on the side of the Dutch, they had no avenue of retreat, for the rebels poured on them that special hatred reserved for traitors; and any attempt to switch sides would have qualified them as traitors to the whites with similar results. The Rangers earned their freedom in this fratricidal struggle not only by fighting with extraordinary courage and élan but by teaching the white troops the art of colonial warfare. According to Captain Stedman, these newly emancipated slaves understood the rudiments of warfare on the Surinam countryside much better than the Dutch army, which had the sense to study the methods of their despised "inferiors."

Although the Bush Negroes—those whose previous successful efforts had won them peace treaties and territory of their own—hated the Rangers and probably sympathized with the rebels, they stood by their treaties and refused to enter the war. In view of the precariousness of the colonials' position before the arrival of reinforcements from Europe, a maroon rising might have tipped the scales decisively and transformed Surinam into an early version of Saint-Domingue.

Brazilian slaves wrote an especially impressive story of guerrilla resistance. In 1770, for example, the Portuguese crushed the *quilombo* of Carlota in Mato Grosso, although the rebels put up, in the words of Raimondo Nina Rodrigues, "a brilliant defense." The most compelling of these maroon war camps arose during the seventeenth century with the name Palmares. For the greater part of a century (*ca*. 1605–1695) runaway slaves and their offspring, swelling to an estimated—if suspiciously high—population of twenty thousand, defended their reconstituted African community against the blows of the Netherlands and Portugal, two of the greatest powers of the age. The Dutch sent two expeditions against Palmares and the Portuguese more than a dozen before they finally crushed it. Slaves had long slipped from the sugar plantations to the backcountry, and Palmares may well have consisted of several discontinuous settlements over time. The movement picked up dramatically in the wake of the Dutch invasion of Pernambuco and the resultant weakening of the Portuguese slaveholders' regime.

The history of Palmares remains obscure despite such excellent studies as those of Edison Carneiro, Ernesto Ennes, and R. K. Kent, and the publication of valuable documents. The sources, unfortunately, betray too much special pleading from the colonial side and offer virtually nothing from the rebel side. As a result, the political and military history of the decisive period, 1672–1695, has emerged, at least in outline, but the social and cultural development of the *quilombo* itself cannot be described without considerable speculation.

In essential respects the Palmarinos seem to have tried to reconstruct an African society. Although blacks from various parts of Africa converged in Palmares, the Bantu-speaking Angolan-Congolese peoples apparently predominated. After a period of reliance on raids for women and supplies, launched against the plantation districts and the Indian settlements of the interior, the Palmarinos began to produce their own food and tools. The *quilombo* became more economically self sufficient and economically complex and supported skilled mechanics and craftsmen. Fragmentary evidence suggests that the economic organization adhered to family-based West African norms.

Politically, the Palmarinos concentrated power in the hands of a small group of chiefs. They practiced a "Catholicism" unconnected with the Church and heavily laden with African beliefs and practices, although little definite is known about the content and organization of this syncretic religion or its place in the political and social system. The Palmarinos' attitude toward slavery itself recalled African origins. They enslaved those whom they had to take from the plantations by force, while welcoming as brothers and sisters those who defected to them. That they practiced traditional African rather than commercial slavery may be extrapolated from the general economic organization and from their willingness to free slaves who volunteered to help raid the plantations.

Until the phase of the long struggle, the Palmarinos apparently spread themselves thin across a large area. For a long time their dispersal of population served them well against the Dutch and Portuguese invasions. The destruction of one or more centers resulted in regroupment and the resumption of a general guerrilla warfare that wore down their enemies. In the last phase, however, the invaders improved their staying power and hammered the Palmarinos piece-meal. The beleaguered Palmarinos concentrated their forces at Macaco, their chief redoubt, but succumbed to the frontal assault of white and Indian troops.

The Palmarinos' success in developing their economy led to an important alliance with some of the neighboring slaveholding planters. In return for guaranties against raiding, some planters entered into trade relations. Whether the Palmarinos returned runaways from certain plantations is not clear. The alliance must always have been shaky, for so long as Palmares existed, it provided a beacon to slaves who dared to risk flight.

In 1678 the regime inflicted heavy losses on the Palmarinos, whose supreme chief, the ganga-zumba, sued for peace. The Portuguese offered terms they considered generous, maybe too generous, including recognition of the freedom of the Palmarinos, appointment of the ganga-zumba as a royal field commander, and confirmation of the Palmarinos' claims to territory already being eyed greedily by planters and merchants. The Palmarinos in return had to give up some territory, return runaways, and help suppress slave and Indian revolts. One group of Palmarinos, under the leadership of the zumbí (war chief) and other younger men, repudiated the agreement, executed the ganga-zumba, and resumed the struggle. Not until 1695 did a powerful coalition of *paulista* ruffians, hastily recruited northerners, and a larger army of Indians, put an end to Palmares. The zumbí, referred to in one Portuguese document as a "Negro of singular courage, great spirit and persistence [negro de singular valor, grande animo e constancia]," was taken alive, although wounded, and subsequently executed.

The zumbí's reasons for repudiating the treaty of 1678 remain open to speculation. Just as some of the Portuguese authorities feared that the Palmarinos would break their word, so the Palmarinos clearly distrusted Portuguese intentions. The rich lands of Palmares had already attracted white interest, and even the limited land cessions provided for by the treaty may have exceeded what the bolder Palmarinos thought safe. Then too, despite their recent victories, the Portuguese had paid dearly for the long war and confronted internal divisions between *paulistas* and northerners and between local planters anxious for peace and others ready for risky adventures. The zumbí may have calculated that the Portuguese would crack during a protracted war, especially since the relations between the *paulistas* and the Indians, who provided an indispensable force, were deteriorating. The zumbí and his followers may have objected to playing policemen for the Portuguese against the slaves. Whatever the reasons, the decision to stake everything on a war to the death ended in death for the rebel leaders and their boldest followers, in the enslavement of many others, and in the division of Palmares among the invading whites. A formidable threat to the Portuguese slaveholding regime had ended.

The Jamaican maroons dated from the 1650s, when the English took the island from Spain. Some slaves took advantage of the struggle between the European powers to fly to the interior, where cool weather offered a healthful climate conducive to the building of stable communities. These early maroon colonies suffered hard military blows and succumbed only to be replaced by others. By the time the Spanish left Jamaica some 1,500 maroons, according to Bryan Edward's shaky estimate, had ensconced themselves in the virtually inaccessible mountainous interior. Their greatest military weakness stemmed from their geographical division, for large groups had occupied different terrain without effective contact. The English, upon consolidating their power, offered one group autonomy in return for support in suppressing slave revolts and in defending the island against invasion.

In time mass defections troubled the English plantation owners, much as they had previously troubled the Spanish. In 1690 the slaves in Clarendon Parish rose in insurrection and retreated into the interior. Those left behind sent the rebels information and supplies from their provision grounds until stable and self-sufficient maroon colonies could take shape. One maroon group, after a period of defeat, united behind Cudjoe, in R. C. Dallas' words, "a bold, skillful, and enterprising man." Steadily reinforced by deserters from the plantations, some of them in large groups, the maroons consolidated community discipline and organized an elaborate intelligence apparatus on the plantations by relying on the obeahmen and those under their influence.

The British governor, Edward Trelawney, read the signs and, in 1738, offered peace terms. Cudjoe kissed the feet of the governor's emissary and begged pardon, although this self prostration, itself probably no more than a traditional courtesy, accompanied assurances that the emissary had brought satisfactory terms. After these maroons agreed to terms then other maroons, under another able leader, Quao, followed suit while making clear that necessity, not preference, dictated their course.

The agreement between Governor Trelawney and Cudjoe —"Articles of Pacification with the Maroons of Trelawney Town, concluded March 1, 1738"—began on a significant note: "In the name of God, amen. Whereas Captain Cudjoe, Captain Accompong, Captain Johnny, Captain Cuffy, Captain Quaco . . ." The governor understood that he was negotiating with "captains," not "niggers." The stated purpose of the treaty was "peace and friendship." It granted freedom and autonomy to the maroons along with possession of designated lands. The maroons obtained hunting rights, as well as the right to cultivate their lands as they wished, but agreed to sell the produce in towns only in accordance with prescribed rules. The maroons agreed to pay homage to the governor; to submit to the jurisdiction of white courts in interracial disputes; and to qualify their control of justice in their own territory by petitioning for white permission to inflict the death penalty. Two white men, appointed by the governor, were to live among the maroons more or less as governors-general; simultaneously, Captain Cudjoe achieved official recognition as an officer of the Crown.

The maroons' most important concessions transcended these ceremonial matters and acquiescence in a measure of extraterritoriality. They agreed to help repel foreign invasion and to return all runaway slaves to their plantations: More ominously:

> Sixth, that the said Captain Cudjoe and his successors do use their best endeavors to take, kill, suppress, or destroy either by themselves, or jointly with any other number of men, commanded on that service by his excellency, the Governor, or commander in chief for the time being, all rebels wheresoever they be, throughout this island, unless they submit to the same terms of accommodation granted to Captain Cudjoe and his successors.

This compromise marked a new stage in the relations of the maroons and the slaves. The earlier alliance, based on slave support for the maroons and maroon efforts to assist runaways, gave way to antagonism. Relations had, however, not proceeded smoothly even during the 1690s and the early eighteenth century, for free Negroes and slaves promised emancipation had provided some of the toughest troops sent against the maroons. The maroons kept their word to the British: They ruthlessly tracked down runaways, killing them so often that the British had to offer a premium for those taken alive; and they smashed new runaway colonies with such efficiency that they jeopardized their own survival, for no significant additions to maroon ranks occurred. And, as Barbara Kopytoff has demonstrated, they opened themselves to a complex process of internal deterioration and a steady erosion of their political cohesion and autonomy. The British authorities had no doubt that the military prowess of the maroons was playing a major role in discouraging slave revolts. Moreover, although the treaty terms forbade the maroons from owning slaves, they did buy some without provoking the intervention of the authorities. Maroons continued to marry slaves and to cultivate sympathetic relations with some, but increasingly the two groups diverged and passed over to animosity.

In 1795 the slaves claimed revenge. Two maroons, generally acknowledged as trouble-makers, fell into British hands and received whippings, which slaves inflicted on behalf of the authorities. The maroons were enraged. They cared nothing for the culprits, whom they themselves would probably have hanged, but they refused to tolerate the use of despised slaves as agents of justice. They reiterated their loyalty to the Crown but demanded, "Do not subject us to insult and humiliation from the very people to whom we are set in opposition." The origins of the rising of the Trelawney maroons remain obscure, although maroon suspicion of changes in British administration, British fears of a new Haiti, stemming in part from reports of French agents among the blacks, and growing quarrels over landholding all played a part. The insulting incident triggered the outbreak of the great Maroon War of 1795–1796, in which the Trelawney maroons had to challenge British power without a mass base of sympathy among the slaves and without even the support of other big maroon groups. The Accompong maroons helped to suppress the rising, as did some slaves whom the British armed for the war. Without help from the plantations, the Trelawney maroons had to fight alone. The rebels, several hundred strong, fought heroically, defied the troops of the world's greatest power, and terrorized a large part of the island. Without adequate allies, however, and facing the threat of vicious dogs from Cuba to be used to hunt them down, they eventually had to sue for peace. The whites had had reason to fear another Saint-Domingue in 1795, for British troops had been sent from Jamaica to suppress slave revolts in the French Caribbean, and unified black action would have had excellent prospects. The policy of divide and rule had triumphed.

Maroons harassed the slaveholders of the Old South from the seventeenth century to the end of their regime. The authorities in Virginia, for example, expressed concern in the 1670s over the possibilities of slave revolt but, even more, concern over the activities of small groups of maroons in every part of the colony. During the eighteenth century the authorities put down a vigorous maroon colony in the Blue Ridge mountains as well as smaller groups but had constant trouble with others in the Dismal Swamp.

The Dismal Swamp area along the Virginia–North Carolina border provided runaways with a favorable location on which to build houses, plant crops, and raise pigs and fowl. Toward the end of the seventeenth century the maroon groups had grown larger and more stable and evoked white fears of a general black insurrection. Punitive expeditions destroyed settlements and kept the runaways from consolidating strong guerrilla bases. By the late antebellum period the maroon problem in the area had shrunk to the status of a nuisance. In Georgia and South Carolina during the eighteenth century a similar pattern unfolded, with small groups of maroons waging sporadic warfare, suffering blows, and regrouping without being able to develop and consolidate major war camps like those of Palmares or the interior colonies of Jamaica, Surinam, or Saint-Domingue.

During the ninteenth century the center of maroon activity shifted to the southwest, especially Louisiana, and to Florida, where the Seminole Indians offered refuge to fleeing blacks and produced a major confrontation with white power. Reports of activity ("outrages," to use the favorite word of the authorities) by small groups of runaways continued to filter in from the seaboard slave states, but they no longer provoked the deep and widespread fear they once had. In the west, maroons in Tennessee caused much concern during the early decades of the nineteenth century, and small groups operated in the Gulf states on a scale just large enough to keep many communities nervous. The peak of nineteenth century maroon activity came during the war, when long hidden groups appeared in full view and many others arose among slaves deserting the plantations. In South Carolina especially, the federal invasion of the coast and the favorable geography of the low country spurred a rash of armed and combative maroon colonies.

The relationship of the black slaves and maroons with the Indians, who controlled parts of the interior and provided an alternative to white domination, helps explain the limited effect of maroon activity in the South. From the earliest days the whites expressed concern about black-Indian collaboration and took measures to prevent it. White fears rested on some evidence of sympathy and mutual support. During the seventeenth and eighteenth centuries various Indian tribes ignored treaty obligations to return runaways and provided refuge for them instead. During the nineteenth century individual runaway slaves and even small groups sought and received protection from some Indian communities especially in the southwestern slave states.

The classic policy of divide and rule poisoned black-Indian relations from the beginning. Mutual sympathy among blacks, Indians, and poor whites had taken root during the colonial period, especially during the seventeenth century, for Indians as well as blacks suffered enslavement and many whites worked as indentured servants under conditions of oppression that sometimes rivaled those of the slaves. From time to time this sympathy flowered into collaboration, but as Indian slavery and white indenture waned, the isolation of the blacks set in. In colonial Virginia under the English and in Louisiana under the French, slaves went into battle against Indians who were fighting an ostensible European advance which in fact was an Afro-European advance all along the frontier. In colonial South Carolina the slaveholders lived in constant dread of Afro-Indian collaboration.

Blacks and Indians did sometimes establish alliances against the whites; in general, however, they remained strangers to each other, divided in their interests and suspicious of each other's strange ways. The whites never wholly succeeded in overcoming their nightmares, but they did succeed in playing the one against the other. Indian troops helped to crush rebellious slaves, and armed slaves helped subdue the Indians. As Gary B. Nash writes in *Red, White, and Black*:

> By fashioning the harshest slave code of any of the colonies, by paying dearly for Indian support at critical moments, and by militarizing their society, white Carolinians were able to restrict the flow of blacks into the backcountry. The Cherokee hill country never became the equivalent of the Maroon hideaways in Jamaica or the Brazilian *quilombos* as a refuge for runaway slaves as many Carolinians feared.

Some slaves won their freedom by fighting on the white side during Indian wars. The employment of black troops against the Indians faded during the late antebellum period only to reemerge on a large scale during the postbellum campaigns in the West. For better or worse, black troops achieved a splendid military record in the federal government's campaigns to crush the last great Indian nations. Thus, we find the Indians' grotesque depiction of the black troops as "black white men." In antebellum times Indians also suffered at the hands of black slaves who acted as spies and translators for white speculators engaged in swindles and land expropriation. The Indians, especially those in South Carolina and Louisiana, returned these compliments by helping to crush slave rebellions and by hunting down runaway slaves. Effective white manipulation of Indians and blacks against each other reduced possibilities for the organization of stable maroon colonies.

More than white manipulation divided Indians from blacks, for they represented different cultures, sometimes appeared almost as strange to each other as to the whites, and had little in common except when, as during the Seminole War, the excesses and tactical blunders of those who oppressed them drove them together.

The Seminole Wars, the most dramatic and significant ventures in black-Indian cooperation against the whites, occurred in Florida, which until its annexation by the United States in 1819, and especially when under the Spanish, had provided a haven for runaway American slaves. The first known slave conspiracy in South Carolina—that of 1720— was inspired by the possibilities presented by Spanish power across the border, and runaways to Florida built forts and colonies during the 1730s. An agreement between Spain and the United States in 1791 to return runaways broke down almost immediately. American efforts to annex Florida in the first decade of the nineteenth century, featured by unsavory plotting with Spanish traitors, resulted in part from a persistent concern with the runaway problem.

Without the cooperation of the Spanish, and for a brief period the English, authorities, the blacks could not easily have established themselves in Florida, but their main reliance fell upon the Seminole Indians. Black runaways built small colonies of their own during the eighteenth and nineteenth centuries within the political framework of the Indian nation. The Seminoles did buy some black slaves in imitation of white practice, but in effect they worked their slaves as dependent share croppers. The blacks slowly insinuated themselves, along with the runaways, into Indian life. When American marines invaded Florida in 1812, Indians and blacks repulsed them in a joint effort that foreshadowed the war to come. American officers then as later regarded the blacks as the toughest and most determined enemies they encountered. The Seminole Wars, caused in no small part by the unwillingness of the Indians to surrender blacks they regarded as part of their own community, pitted blacks as well as Indians against the whites, who had some free Negro allies of their own. Some blacks assumed commanding positions in the Seminole military effort. They fought so tenaciously that the American authorities bluntly characterized the war as primarily a struggle against black maroons and their Indian allies.

The Second Seminole War (1835) cost the American military 1,600 lives, with many more wounded, as well as a staggering thirty to forty million dollars. The United States had won another of its wars, but not without the galling admission that it could not wholly impose its will on the Afro-Indian alliance. The Americans had to make the major concession of allowing the blacks to move west with the Seminoles. In its scope and heroism the black struggle deserves to rank with that of the maroons of Jamaica or Surinam, although it did not make nearly so great an impact on the wider slave society.

The magnificent unity of the blacks and Seminoles had precedents, the most notable of which was the black support for the great rising of the Natchez in Louisiana in 1729. In the aftermath of that event, the whites moved to placate the blacks and drive a wedge between them and their Indian allies. They scored some success, but, as the conspiracy at Pointe Coupee demonstrated anew in 1795, the threat of black-Indian cooperation remained acute so long as the French and Spanish held Louisiana.

The struggle of the blacks and Seminoles in any case did not have the electrifying impact on the plantation South it might have, for the hard blows delivered by the whites kept the blacks and Seminoles on the defensive. The American authorities and the southern slaveholders appreciated the magnitude of the threat, for the Florida colonies posed more than a direct military thrust and a beacon to escaping slaves. The existence of autonomous black communities—the degree of their cultural autonomy within the Seminole political structure remains unclear—created the danger of an alternative black society. Time and circumstance—and brute force —did not, however, permit the example to spread.

Black-Indian contacts included Indian slaveownership and miscegenation. Indians held black slaves in considerable numbers: During the 1820s and 1830s Indians ranked as some of Georgia's biggest slaveholders, and subsequently Greenwood Leflore, the half-white Choctaw chief, emerged as one of Mississippi's biggest planters with four hundred slaves. John Ross, the famous Cherokee chief, owned about one hundred slaves in 1860. By 1860 black slaves comprised 12.5 percent of the population of the Indian Territory, although most lived on small farms. Some Indians, notably the Chicasaws, had a reputation as hard masters, but most enjoyed a reputation among whites and blacks for being generous, kind, and easy-going. The Creeks, in particular, often worked their slaves in arrangements more suggestive of share-cropping than slavery and sometimes adopted them into the tribe. The Cherokees and some other Indians made alliances with the Confederacy, although an exposed geographical position and Byzantine factional politics largely determined their decision.

The narratives of ex-slaves contain many assertions of Indian ancestry. Some of these may have reflected a wish to dissociate from African ancestry or to reduce its importance, but many gave no hint of lack of black pride and appear matter of fact. Other reports spoke more generally of contacts between slaves and Indians as a normal feature of life. For example, George Fortman, an Indian enslaved in Alabama, said that many presumed black slaves had been Indians like himself and that the blacks responded with considerable kindness and made him comfortable. Court records, travelers' accounts, and other sources make clear that, in fact, black-Indian miscegenation occurred frequently and that every community had some slaves with Indian ancestry.

These changing cultural relationships of blacks and Indians had profound political repercussions. Some Indian communities became utterly transformed by the entrance of large numbers of blacks, but, typically, the communities absorbed black slaves and runaways into their own culture and social organization. Males predominated among runaways, and marriage to Indian women usually followed as a matter of course. Among the Creeks and other Indian tribes that adhered to the principle of matrilineal descent, absorption of blacks into Indian culture proceeded the more rapidly, and they rose to positions of considerable tribal influence. Since the larger Indian slaveholders usually were part white and these acted as the Indian communities' most determined agents of acculturation and assimilation to white norms, their slaves could not easily develop Afro-American cultural patterns of their own.

In short, whether the blacks entered Indian communities as slaves or free men, they could not reconstruct an Afro-American world or construct an Indo-African one. No doubt they imparted something to Indian culture and transmitted some features of Indian culture to Afro-America, but for the most part they either became Indians, in essential cultural respects, or stood in the same relationship to rapidly acculturating, semi-white Indian slaveholders that they did to white slaveholders. Indian refuge for runaway slaves provided little or no opportunity for the flowering of an Afro-American alternative to plantation slavery and might, therefore, have reduced the chances for large-scale black maroon activity. The great centers of maroon activity—Palmares, the Jamaican mountains, eastern Saint-Domingue and Cuba, Surinam —either had few Indians or Indians so hostile as to throw the blacks entirely on their own resources.

The geographic dimension deserves closer study, but, as Bennett Wall has observed, the terrain of the Old South put unusual difficulties in the way of would-be maroons, or at least of those who aspired to form large-scale maroon communities. Great swamps did exist, and so did many fastnesses within 150 miles of the coast from Virginia to Louisiana. Indeed, those regions housed bands of white and black outlaws long after the war. The most favorable terrain, however, was in Florida, where individuals and small groups could lose themselves. And as research continues, we do find evidence of more and more small maroon groups. But, again with the exception of Florida, the very geographic isolation and limited means of subsistence drastically reduced both the possibilities for large-scale maroon concentrations—for a North American Palmares—and for decisive military-political intervention in the greater slave society. The question concerns less the existence of *marronage*—it did exist—than of *marronage* on a scale that could affect the politics of the slave society, especially the politics inherent in any encouragement to slave revolt, in a manner comparable to that in Brazil, Jamaica, Surinam, or even Colombia or Venezuela. The slaves of the Old South did not, in any case, always look upon their own local runaway groups with favor and sometimes helped to suppress them. The runaways, often called "outlyers," typically huddled in small units and may be called "maroons" only as a courtesy. They occupied unfavorable terrain with only minimum security and rarely had an opportunity to forge a viable community life. Consequently, many degenerated into wild desperadoes who preyed on anyone, black, white, or red, in their path. A slave told Olmsted that you could always tell a swamp runaway by his appearance: He would likely be frightened, emaciated, and indecently clothed even by slave standards.

Other slaves and ex-slaves left an unattractive picture of parasites, thieves, and murderers who plagued the quarters as readily as the Big House. Julia Blanks and Green Cumby of Texas described local swamp runaways as mean, frightening, wild men who terrorized the slaves into supplying them with food. "And if you didn't do it," said Mrs. Blanks, "if they ever got you they sure would fix you." According to H. C. Bruce, in his book *The New Man*, slaves often refused to betray organized runaways not because of a sense of solidarity but because of fear of ghastly reprisals. Such reports from black sources make understandable the claims in white sources that slaves often caught or reported runaways, from whom they often suffered heavy depredations. In 1857, for example, Eliza Magruder of Mississippi recorded in her diary:

Two runaways from Claiborne rode in the yard and went in the kitchen and cooked and ate supper. Afterwards went into

Fred's house and made up and baked biscuit. Made up a bundle to carry off when the bread was done. Then went to bed to wait for it. He was taken by the servants and carried to the Hospital and put in the stocks. It seems they have been committing depredations through the neighborhood.

In many other cases the slaves helped groups of runaways and identified with their plight. Some planters complained bitterly about the support that the slaves extended to these groups, even hiding them on the plantations. If the runaways had originated in the immediate area and had friends, they could readily expect help. If not, they might gain support by soliciting rather than stealing from the slaves, by avoiding acts of terror, and by appealing to the slaves' sympathy.

Too often, however, the maroons displayed many of the socially destructive and only some of the socially positive features of banditry in general. Rural outlaws, hunted as criminals by the regime, may remain within peasant society as heroes, champions, and avengers. Romance aside, they do often prey on the poor as well as the rich but often will not prey on the poor of their own immediate neighborhoods. Normally, they understand the extent to which they must rely on the sympathy and affection of their own people in order to procure supplies, shelter, and, above all, silence. But since these bandits take their fate into their own hands they cannot easily avoid a certain contempt for the passive masses. They can spring to support a peasant or slave uprising but do not necessarily exude much concern during more placid times.

The degeneration of some runaways into desperadoes who preyed on black and white alike illuminates one of the many anomalies inherent in the southern maroon experience. Clovis

Moura, in his valuable book *Rebeliões da senzala*, provides a good analysis of the military price paid by the Brazilian *quilombolos*, especially those of Palmares, for their socioeconomic consolidation. As the *quilombolos* succeeded in organizing production—in cultivating the land to sustain a large community—they generally lost much of their military flexibility, for they had to give up hit-and-run tactics in order to defend their families, homes, and livelihood. Thus, while increasing numbers made possible sturdier defense against frontal assault, they also compelled direct engagement with such assault. Without a mass population of peasants to melt into, in the manner of classical guerrilla warfare, the choices reduced to two: hit-and-run attacks from small bases that could not feed themselves and periodically required dangerous forward movements; or commitment to the stand-up defense of redoubts. The first tactic worked well for small groups. The second became indispensable for large *quilombos* while making them vulnerable to the superior firepower of their enemies. In Florida the second tactic ended in defeat, although not total defeat. Elsewhere, the second tactic commended itself under generally unfavorable conditions. Only with difficulty, if at all, could groups of runaways avoid that parasitical existence which must eventually alienate rebels from their potential mass base.

The maroons of the Caribbean and South America also displayed both tendencies, but those of the United States did so under circumstances that weakened the positive and increased the negative features of their relationship to the slaves. The maroons of the United States rarely could play the protective role assumed by those of Palmares, Jamaica, or Surinam. Where the police power of the regime faltered or, what came to the same thing, the maroons spread their power over a geographical area ostensibly dominated by the slaveholders, even the blacks who remained slaves had some protection against the excesses of their masters. In the United States the police power remained overwhelming, and the maroons found themselves constantly on the defensive, without much to offer the slaves as *quid pro quo* for information, supplies, and silence. Since the slaves often tended to identify with blacks from their own plantation community—an identification rebel leaders struggled to overcome—even maroons who avoided plundering them could seem dangerous interlopers.

Yet, the maroons made invaluable contributions to the slaves' struggles for a better life in slavery and especially for escape from slavery. Even H. C. Bruce, the ex-slave who wrote so harshly of maroon terrorism against the quarters, acknowledged that those who deserted the plantations and took to the woods compelled masters to treat their slaves better, if only from fear of even heavier losses of capital and labor. Less tangibly, the maroons provided a constant reminder that slaves could flee and even offer armed resistance to the master class. Whatever their limitations, the maroons failed the slaves primarily in the abstract sense of being too few to provide the kind of spark to rebellion so much in evidence elsewhere in the hemisphere.

The more favorable conditions faced by the maroons in Brazil, Jamaica, Surinam, or Saint-Domingue suggest the special difficulties faced by those of the Old South. R. C. Dallas told us much when he closed his history of the Jamaican Maroon War by recommending that free white farmers be settled in the interior. "Let them depend upon their own labour," he wrote, "and let their employment of negroes be very limited. . . . The great object of the scheme is, in the first, a large white population in the interior trained to arms; and in the next, the opening of roads." Reviewing the general history of social banditry, Eric Hobsbawm, in *Primitive Rebels*, adds that the construction of good and fast modern roads alone often undermines banditry. The slave states met these challenges during the nineteenth century. White farmers, armed and stable, constituted a majority of the population and infested most of the South's hills and back country. As the frontier moved west, the terrain favorable to maroons and guerrillas shrank steadily. The military question, then, concerned not merely terrain but the human beings inhabiting it. John Brown, who had taken inspiration and instruction from the experience of the Jamaican maroons, missed the point to his cost when he envisioned impregnable guerrilla bases in the Allegheny Mountains. Long before Harpers Ferry he planned to secure these bases with the support of dissident poor mountain whites, whose racism he seems to have underestimated and whose ideology and politics he certainly misjudged.

The maroons of the United States wrote heroic pages and made a vital contribution to the black struggle against slavery, but under the circumstances their impact had to remain modest. Even those Indian settlements that provided refuge for blacks absorbed them in such a way as to separate them from the slaves culturally as well as physically. By the end of the eighteenth century the danger that large-scale maroon activity would trigger significant slave revolts had passed, although neither maroon activity itself nor white fears ever did.

THREE

The
Turning
Point

Until Afro-American slave revolts and maroon movements merged with the trans-Atlantic bourgeois-democratic revolutions of the late eighteenth century, they looked toward the restoration of as much of a traditional African way of life as could be remembered and copied. More accurately, they looked toward the consolidation of a circumscribed Afro-American world that remained "traditional" in its minimum engagement with the politics, economy, and ideology of the emerging bourgeois world. They resembled in this respect the slave revolts of the ancient world and the many peasant revolts of medieval and early modern Europe, which also struggled for some kind of perceived restoration and lacked the material base and concomitant ideology for the projection of a new and economically more advanced society.

Since in the strictly historical sense all such movements assumed the form of restorationist rebellions, they assumed the superficial aspect of "reactionary" impediments to the development of the productive forces. Many social movements that arose by counterposing a "reactionary" outlook to the tendency of capital to destroy traditional lower-class life in the name of economic progress learned in the course of struggle to formulate demands which foreshadowed new social relations. Conversely, the most revolutionary movements against capital have had to come to terms with older values in order to secure a mass base.

From the beginning, these movements made vital contributions to the democratization of the modern world, for every popular revolt, no matter how much encrusted in backward-looking ideology and objectively dangerous to the development of the productive forces of society, has helped to establish the claims of the people against their oppressors and against those who would use them as pawns even in a historically progressive cause. In the unfolding of the blacks' complex struggle, the early slave revolts—to the extent to which they remained imprisoned in the early maroon vision—developed in a way not merely contradictory but tragic.

The slave revolts of the sixteenth and seventeenth centuries burst upon the world during an epoch of revolutionary change in the mode of production. Slavery arose in the New World in response to the demands of an emerging world market commanded from northwest Europe. Even such fundamentally seigneurial regimes as those of Spain and Portugal expanded westward and built plantation economies in response to the ramifications and strains of the rise of capitalism in Europe. Especially during the seventeenth century they increasingly had to compete militarily, politically, and economically with the emergent bourgeois powers of England and the Netherlands. A general crisis of European seigneurial society, accompanied by major disruptions in the commercial economy, marked the seventeenth century as an era of international turmoil and profound transformation. Everything touched by the force of a self-contradictory European expansion felt the shock.

However far removed from the revolt of the *comuneros* or the *germanía* in Spain or the revolutionary struggles in England and Holland, not to mention the less dramatic manifestations of the European crisis, slavery and black resistance to it constituted part of a single historical movement. The brutal treatment that drove thousands of slaves to flee the sugar plantations for the acute dangers of the interior had its origin, in part, in the pressures to raise the rate of exploitation in the face of stiffening economic demands within a developing world market. And however traditional or backward-looking the world of the Palmarinos, every blow they struck at the Dutch and the Portuguese forced some slight alteration in the course of European capitalism. Whether they knew or cared, the rebellious blacks of Brazil and of the whole hemisphere had become actors on a world historical stage.

The early slave insurgents and maroons shared their restorationist focus with great peasant and artisan movements throughout history. Not all early popular movements had a restorationist character but so many did as to suggest its dominance among Europeans who confronted the early manifestations of a money economy and among those Asians, Africans, and Latin Americans who confronted the later manifestations of colonialism. Peasants, artisans, and even sections of traditional ruling classes periodically raised the banner of restoration in an effort to combat the dissolution of their communities and ways of life and to repeal the new exactions and expropriations inherent in the advance of social relationships based on the cash nexus rather than on familiar patterns of reciprocal duties and responsibilities. The common people of Agen did nothing unusual when they rose against the king's tax collectors (*gabeleurs*) in 1635 under the slogan, "Death to the *gabeleurs*! Kill the *gabeleurs*! Long live the King without *gabelles!*" Michael Cherniavsky, in *Tsar and People*, writes of the great peasant and Cossack risings in Russia from those of the Time of Troubles in the sixteenth century through that of Stenka Razin in the seventeenth to that of Pugachev in the eighteenth, and beyond:

> Nearly all the peasant rebellions during the interregnum of the Time of the Troubles advanced under the banner of the Tsar, utilizing for that purpose the most unlikely pretenders to the throne. . . . The masses were not rebelling against the tsar; if Pugachev is any example, such a conception was unimaginable. They were marching behind their own Orthodox popular Tsar.

The restorationist vision gave way in Saint-Domingue, where the slaves of the New World wrote their most glorious chapter in the midst of a booming sugar industry that had created the world's richest colony. The slaves, in an uneasy and inconsistent alliance with a large minority of propertied mulattoes, defeated the Spanish, inflicted a defeat of unprecedented proportions on the British, and then made their country the graveyard of Napoleon's magnificent army as well as of his imperial ambitions in the New World. In the end, the Americas had their first black national state.

The story of that magnificent revolution, which C. L. R. James has recounted with literary and analytic power, need here concern us only in its bare outlines. The colony had half a million slaves, brutally driven in the midst of an extraordinary economic boom presided over by a class of slaveholders who, when not absentees, wished they were. Of these slaves, at least half and probably two-thirds had come from Africa. Their religion, Vodûn, although it later merged with Catholicism, remained close to its eclectic African origins during the slave period and became a creed of opposition to the white regime and its official religion. Macendal, who has been described as a Muslim, led the most important early resistance movement, and Boukman, a Vodûn priest, led the rising that sparked the great revolution itself.

Many of the leaders who emerged during the revolution came from the privileged slave strata. Toussaint had risen to the position of foreman and could read and write, although not well. Henry Christophe had worked as a hotel waiter and had had some military experience. Those who led the mulatto rising in the south were cultured and sophisticated men of property, not slaves at all. The early leaders of the black revolution in the north, Jean-François and Biassou, had established careers in the military campaigns on the Spanish border. The revolutionaries had behind them knowledge of protracted maroon warfare in the eastern part of the island.

Finally, the ruling class split asunder. The planters and *petits blancs* fought each other and together conspired to keep the mulattoes, many of them rich slaveholders, in racial subordination. The white and mulatto colonials resisted the French bourgeoisie and state, which milked them in the slave trade as well as in an imposed system of unequal trade and tariffs. The metropolitan power crumbled after 1789, and the colonials scampered to choose the winning side and to use events in France to advantage against each other. The arrival of revolutionary French troops, with *liberté, égalité, fraternité* on their lips, hardly helped the slaveholders' cause. And then the white powers fell on each other and bid for black and mulatto support. Toussaint and his generals brilliantly played one ruling-class group against the other and, in the end, made themselves masters of all. In short, Saint-Domingue witnessed the conjuncture of ideal preconditions for slave revolt.

The great revolution marked the turning point in the history of slave revolts in the New World. The people of Saint-Domingue successively humiliated the Spanish, British, and French and inflicted some of the heaviest losses those supreme imperialists ever suffered. Neither Pitt nor Napoleon could have taken much solace from the propaganda that later passed for history, according to which the tropical climate and disease, not black heroism, destroyed their armies. Nor could Napoleon and later Hitler have found the Russian winter a more palatable conqueror than the Russian people. The legends, nonetheless, die hard if at all. Herr Goebbels insisted to the end that the Russian winter accounted for the Nazi defeat in Russia. Some historians continue to agree, notwithstanding such minor details as the great battle of Kursk—"the Nazi Waterloo," as it is accurately called by Soviet historians—which claimed a half million German casualties. Stalin chose to attack during the summer of 1943 in part because he wanted the world to know that his army could do without the snow and cold.

The revolutionary army in Saint-Domingue might in fact have succumbed to the heavier French firepower, yellow fever or no, if it had not been supported by an indomitable mass movement that turned defeats into victories. As the French advanced, writes C. L. R. James, the "people burned San Domingo flat so that at the end of the war it was a charred desert." And as David Brion Davis pointedly remarks in *The Problem of Slavery in the Age of Revolution*:

No doubt Haitian independence, like that of the United States and the Latin American republics, depended upon a variety of circumstances. But if the black population had been easily subdued, the yellow fever epidemic would have made little difference. Both sides knew that the fever would come, like the tropical rains, but only the blacks used the knowledge to their own advantage.

Haiti's emergence meant much more than a major black victory over whites and the creation of a black state. Both had precedents. The maroons of Jamaica, Surinam, and even Saint-Domingue, among others, had defeated the whites and large, autonomous black communities—if not quite "states" —had arisen in Palmares and the back country of several countries. Haiti's special significance rested on more than the greater magnitude of its revolution, its victory, and its emergent territorial state. If the British, French, Dutch, Spanish, and Portuguese could come to terms with large maroon colonies and use them to help crush slave revolts, why should they tremble so at an oversized maroon colony in the middle of the Caribbean?

The revolution under Toussaint, a leader of genius, did not aspire to restore some lost African world or build an isolated Afro-American enclave that, whatever its cultural merit, could have played no autonomous role in world affairs and would have had to become a protectorate of one or another European power. Toussaint, and after his death Dessalines and Henry Christophe, tried to forge a modern black state, based on an economy with a vital export sector oriented to the world market. The ultimate failure of their basically Jacobin program ushered in one of history's most grimly ironical counterrevolutions. Pétion's and Boyer's political relaxation and land reform replaced Henry Christophe's iron dictatorship and maintenance of the sugar plantations under rigorous work discipline. Haiti slowly became, in Sidney Mintz's words, "The Caribbean area's most thoroughgoing peasant country."

Mintz writes in *Caribbean Transformations* of the postrevolutionary Haitian peasantry: "The land is invested with considerable affect: gods live in it; it is the ultimate security against privation; family members are buried in it; food and wealth come from it; and it is good in itself, even if not cultivated." Mintz remarks on the slave-bred land hunger and adds that the peasants remain devoted to the land even when "uneconomical." And, he notes, the peasants absorbed the French revolutionary tradition of agrarian egalitarianism with the disastrous effect of decreasing plot sizes and increasing poverty.

Thus, Haiti slipped into a system of peasant proprietorship and self sufficiency—wonderful euphemisms for the poverty and wretchedness of bourgeois-egalitarian swindles —and the dream of a modern black state drowned in the tragic hunger of an ex-slave population for a piece of land and a chance to live in old ways or ways perceived as old. The Haitian peasants, like the French, turned toward a centralized authoritarian state to protect their hard-won claims to independent proprietorship. But the Haitian state did not have to tread easy in the face of a powerful and dangerous bourgeoisie; much less did it have to support the programmatic aspirations of that bourgeoisie—to advance, as the French state did even if reluctantly, the cause of capitalist development.

The counterrevolution of peasant property in Haiti came

later and, like most counterrevolutions, could not undo the essentials. For a decade and more the Haitian revolution proclaimed something new to Afro-America, as the American and French revolutions had to Euro-America. More accurately, these revolutions formed a single process that spoke to the whole world and signaled the beginning of a new era. The French Revolution, especially the Jacobinism that reshaped the course of history despite the defeat of Robespierre and Saint-Just, would have developed differently had the colonial question, posed with special urgency in Saint-Domingue, not intervened. The Haitian Revolution, in contradistinction to one more rising of slaves, would have been unthinkable without the French Revolution. The blacks of Saint-Domingue did not need the white Jacobins of Paris to teach them to fight for freedom, and the white Jacobins of Paris did not learn the demand for equality from the blacks of Saint-Domingue. But the revolutionary ideology that emerged in the 1790s was fed from both sides of the Atlantic. It Africanized France in ways that helped send the colonialist Girondists to a well deserved fate; it Europeanized Saint-Domingue in ways that pointed toward the rise of a modern black state. But this process went only so far. The Napoleonic counterrevolution restored slavery in the remaining French colonies, and the Pétioniste counterrevolution completed Haiti's isolation. For the first time, however, a slave revolt had become a great national revolution and a vital part of the historical process that irrevocably remade the entire world.

The rise of the world market, manifested politically in the struggle for world power among the stronger European nations, decisively undermined the restorationist threat of peasant and slave movements, for it brought to a close the possibility of political and cultural isolation. No matter how much autonomy and autarchy a maroon community might achieve, it could not isolate itself wholly or avoid playing a political role in the shaping of the modern world. If it came to terms with the regime, as in Jamaica, then its role might have brutally reactionary features, but not without an opposite feature guaranteed by its very existence as a free black enclave amidst a slave population. If it continued to wage war, then it gave direct assistance to the struggle of the enslaved laboring classes against the most barbarous forms of expioitation ushered in by the developing world market. Thus, even the more extreme restoration impulses contributed something to the emergent struggle of the laboring classes against the exploitation and oppression of capital.

So long as the slave revolts aspired to a restoration, however, their contribution to world politics, although never trivial, remained secondary, at the level of effects derived from the objective working-out of a defensive movement. Successfully insurgent slaves either had to restore a lost world, or as much of it as they could, or push into the world of modern, essentially bourgeois social relations. Every slave class in insurrection set for itself the task of self-liquidation —if not for the liquidation of the class as a whole through the total abolition of slavery, then at least for the liquidation of its own particular segment. The path of restoration meant the establishment of essentially primitive-communal social relations, which could never generate political power capable of sustaining genuine autonomy in a world of technologically advanced nation-states. The great maroon communities sank into the category of protectorates to their old enemies or remained guerrilla bases vainly struggling to survive outside the mainstream of history.

Toussaint's vision provided the radical alternative of a modern nation with embryonic modern social relations. Toussaint's revolution called for the "Europeanization" of Saint-Domingue in the same way that it sought to compel the European revolution to come to terms with the aspirations of the colonial peoples. It did not seek to turn the blacks of Saint-Domingue into Europeans but to lead them toward a recognition that European technology had revolutionized the world and forced all peoples to participate in the creation of a world culture at once nationally variegated and increasingly uniform. From that moment, the slaves of the New World had before them the possibility of a struggle for freedom that pointed toward participation in the mainstream of world history rather than away from it.

The international bourgeois-democratic revolution of the last quarter of the eighteenth century opened in America and crested in France. But it had a profound impact throughout the Americas and, in its Haitian manifestation, had an impact on Afro-America that transcended the political and ideological shaping of the black struggle for justice. It helped prepare Afro-America's forcible intervention in world politics. Those who worship at the feet of the gods of Power may see elites as the sole movers of history, but the great personalities of those elites, who sometimes deserve the respect they get as a matter of superstition, have generally learned from galling experience that the most abject of subjects sooner or later claim their price. "I have to reproach myself," moaned the fallen Napoleon Bonaparte when it was too late, "with the attempt made upon the colony during my consulship. The design of reducing it by force was a great error. I ought to have been satisfied with governing it through the medium of Toussaint."

The mighty Napoleon and the proud planters of South Carolina had a rough awakening: "The role which the great Negro Toussaint, called L'Ouverture, played in the history of the United States," W. E. B. Du Bois wrote almost eighty years ago, as might be written even now despite C. L. R. James's great book, "has seldom been appreciated." Developing a line of thought opened by Henry Adams, he argued that the revolution in Saint-Domingue enormously strengthened the antislavery movement in England and prepared the way for its flowering in America; that it ended Napoleon's dream of an American empire and led him to the sale of Louisiana, which doubled the size of the United States; and that it influenced, perhaps decisively, the decision of the southern states to close the African slave trade. In these as in so many other ways, Haiti became, in the words Raúl Castro used for Cuba in our own day, a small country with a big revolution.

The interlocking French and Haitian revolutions shattered the tranquillity, such as it was, of the slaveholding regions everywhere in the hemisphere and generated rational fear among the slaveholders. They stirred the slaves and free Negroes to rebellion under a modern ideology that posed a new and more dangerous threat to the old regimes than anything previously encountered. That threat declined after the collapse of Toussaint's rapprochement with France and Napoleon's brutal attempt to re-enslave the island. During the 1790s, however, the interest of the revolutionaries of Paris in breaking the counterrevolutionary power of England and

Spain, not to mention of their own Girondists, resulted in efforts, often carried by French-speaking blacks, to encourage slave revolts and movements for national liberation.

Even when the counterrevolution in France had given way to a moribund Bourbon Restoration and when the promise of Haitian revolution had faded, the ideas of the revolutionary epoch haunted the slave regimes. During the nineteenth century the traditional-restorationist ideologies of the early slave revolts gave way before a new bourgeois-democratic ideology, which imparted to subsequent slave revolts a new quality and power. Refugees from Saint-Domingue spread all over the Caribbean, the northern coast of South America, and South Carolina and Louisiana, taking their slaves with them. Those slaves had seen and heard much during the revolutionary conflagration, and everywhere they became carriers of new doctrines. The slaveholders of Trinidad had dealt with recalcitrant slaves before, but now they had to deal with those wearing the Tricolor and singing the Marseillaise, which however French in form carried an internationalist content. The difference neither was nor was perceived to be trivial. In Venezuela, during the big slave revolt at Coro in 1795 and again during the revolt of 1798, the rebels, reported to be in touch with revolutionary French and Italian sailors, proclaimed "the law of the French, the Republic, liberty for the slaves," and an end to economic and social injustices. As Spanish South America moved into a struggle for national independence, influenced by democratic ideas, during the Napoleonic Wars, slaves and free Negroes fought in large numbers on both sides. Initially, the royalists offered freedom to slaves who volunteered to fight, but the return to power of the reactionary Ferdinand VII undermined the policy and gave the patriots the chance to make the issue their own. Increasingly, black participation assured the patriot armies victory and put the institution of slavery on borrowed time. As would happen in Cuba during the second half of the nineteenth century, a vast war for national independence became the principal spur to emancipation of the slaves.

The intersection of American expansion into Louisiana with the closing of the African slave trade decisively shaped the subsequent history of the slaveholders' regime, which faced the formidable task of expanding its slave force to meet the imminent demand of the new regions of the Southwest. Thus, the train of events that Dr. Du Bois saw propelled by the revolution in Saint-Domingue extended much further and compelled the general amelioration of the material conditions of slave life. Toussaint could not liberate the slaves of the South, but he did contribute to their living in a more humane framework with room to develop their own cultural resources.

Gabriel Prosser in 1800 and Denmark Vesey in 1822 consciously looked to Haiti for inspiration and support, and as late as 1840 slaves in South Carolina were interpreting news from Haiti as a harbinger of their own liberation. This is not to say that Gabriel Prosser or Denmark Vesey necessarily valued the revolution in Saint-Domingue, however they interpreted its specifics, more highly than they valued the American Revolution—we just do not know. Rather, for them, the self-liberation of slaves of Saint-Domingue represented the full realization of those ideals of the American Revolution which they respected and indeed appealed to. In

1800, Representative Rutledge of South Carolina told Congress that the slaves already had felt "this new-fangled French philosophy of liberty and equality." And in the aftermath of the Vesey plot, Edwin Clifford Holland described the blacks as "Jacobins":

> Let it never be forgotten that our Negroes are freely the *Jacobins* of the country; that they are the *Anarchists* and the *Domestic* Enemy: the *common enemy of civilized society*, and the *barbarians* who *would if they could, become the destroyers of our race*.

The slaveholders, however, quick to exaggerate, had not become paranoid; they understood the potential of what they saw. References to the example and inspiration of Haiti reverberated across black America. The impact on David Walker may be readily seen from his great *Appeal*. Haiti, William Watkins told a meeting of free Negroes in Baltimore in 1825, provides "an irrefutable argument to prove that the descendants of Africa were never designed by their creator to sustain an inferiority, or even a mediocrity in the chain of being." And the slaveholders were not amused by celebrations of Haitian independence such as that staged in 1859 by free Negro masons in St. Louis, Missouri—a slave state. Jefferson had noted, "The West Indies appears to have given considerable impulse to the minds of the slaves . . . in the United States." The revolution in Saint-Domingue propelled a revolution in black consciousness throughout the New World.

The extent to which the revolution in Saint-Domingue fired the imagination of the southern slaves remains a matter of conjecture, but some telling signs command attention. Notably, in the middle of the nineteenth century the slaves in

Louisiana were heard singing revolutionary songs first heard in the early days of the revolution in Saint-Domingue. Nor should Haiti's impact on the black abolitionists be slighted. During the nineteenth century, especially during 1840–1860, many black leaders established contact with Haiti, as well as with Africa, and many more took heart from the revolutionary experience there. The links between these developments and the underground railroad and the subsequent work of northern blacks among the freedmen need further study, but the discernible overlapping of personnel demonstrates the existence of those links. *L'Union*, a bilingual newspaper published by free Negroes in New Orleans, chose carefully the images invoked to call for black-colored unity in response to the Emancipation Proclamation:

> Brothers! The hour strikes for us; a new sun, similar to that of 1789, should surely appear on our horizon. May the cry which resounded through France at the seizure of the Bastille resonate today in our ears. . . . Let us all be imbued with these noble sentiments which characterize all civilized people. . . . In sweet accord with our brothers, let us fill the air with these joyous cries: "vive la liberté! vive l'union! vive la justice pour tous les hommes!"

The Haitians who directly or indirectly encouraged American blacks to rebel against slavery paid off an old debt. After all, they owed America much. Of Count d'Estaing's 3,600 French troops at Savannah in 1779, 545 were blacks. To be sure, they participated primarily as servants and menials. But they had eyes, ears, and brains and could judge events for themselves. One of them was Henry Christophe.

The shift from a restorationist toward a bourgeois-democratic ideology reflected deepening changes in the ethnic character of the slave revolts. African-born slaves, especially those recently imported, and creole slaves constituted the two great groups everywhere, but the Africans often organized themselves into competing groups based on their ethnic origins. Both slaveholders and abolitionists regarded the Africans as much more dangerous and revolt-prone than the creoles, who developed a not entirely fair reputation as accommodationists.

Before the nineteenth century, when creole slaves introduced a new and fateful political content into the history of slave revolts, the Africans organized and executed the vast majority of revolts and certainly the major ones. From such early risings as that of the Wolofs on Hispaniola in 1522 to the war in Palmares, to the rising on St. John in 1733, to the great Jamaican risings of the eighteenth century, to the series of revolts that shook Bahia during the first four decades of the nineteenth century, Africans predominated everywhere.

The usual explanation falls on the warlike character of many African peoples and their difficulty in adjusting to life as slaves and to the accommodationism inherent in the creoles' having been born into slavery and having no personal experience with freedom. This explanation does the creoles an injustice. Since the slave trade to the Americas remained wide open until the beginning of the nineteenth century and open to Cuba and Brazil long after and since the slaves outside British North America did not reproduce themselves, African-born slaves had to predominate. As a result, the accommodationism of the creoles may have flowed less from their easier adjustment to slavery than from their cultural distance from and even antipathy to the Africans, no doubt complicated by the creoles' access to more privileged positions on the plantations and in the towns and cities. A revolt that aspired to the restoration of an African way of life could have little appeal for creoles who had become partially European in their emergence as Afro-Americans. The hostility between Africans and creoles did not arise, as is often alleged, from the militancy of the one and the docility of the other. In specific cases the creoles assumed the role of fighters and the Africans that of supporters of the regime. After slavery, this reversal became particularly evident. In British Guiana, for example, the creoles led big strikes after emancipation while the Africans worked as scabs. The nature of the several black communities required different kinds of struggles, and interethnic cooperation, which when effected produced impressive movements, remained difficult to achieve.

Ethnic rivalry divided some Africans from others as readily as Africans from creoles. Fierce antagonisms developed in Cuba, Brazil, Jamaica, Saint-Domingue, and other places between the Bantu-speaking slaves from the Angola-Congo region and the Sudanic-speaking slaves from Guinea. Slave revolts failed in several countries because of ethnic animosities. In 1724, for example, Angolan (*bantu*) and Yoruba (*nagô*) slaves rose separately in Minas Gerais, Brazil, since they could not agree on a single leader, whereas a joint effort might have succeeded. Although colonialist policy had generally tried to throw different African peoples together, sometimes it went into reverse. Some Brazilian officials saw the advantage in grouping African peoples separately, for although the danger of ethnic conflict would increase, the more formidable danger of general slave revolt would decrease. Regardless of official policy the slaves often found ways to group themselves along traditional lines.

Actual ethnic origins did not necessarily determine events in ethnic slave rebellions. In Jamaica and the British Caribbean generally the "Coromantine" (Akan) slaves repeatedly led the great slave rebellions until the nineteenth century. But many and perhaps even most of those so-called Coromantines may have been other peoples who fell under the sway of the most prestigious group and identified with its strength. Slaves who came from Africa on the same ship retained quasi-familial relations in the New World, and the highly respected Ashanti warriors no doubt commanded special respect during the long voyage. The Ashanti sometimes did yeoman work for the whites as virtual *Kapos* on the slave ships and as drivers and later policemen in the islands. Yet, the same qualities that led them into those roles also made them the most feared of all slave revolutionaries. Not surprisingly, many slaves of different origins wanted to assimilate to the Coromantines and willingly followed them into battle. In Jamaica, as in Bahia where the Hausa and Yoruba who had fought each other in Africa joined to foment the great nineteenth-century risings, ethnic solidarity could become a powerful force. Ethnic solidarity often depended on the extent to which one African people had the strength to impose its hegemony on the others and on the extent to which the Africans as a group heavily outnumbered the creoles.

The role of the creoles in the British Caribbean changed dramatically with the shift in the creole-African balance during the nineteenth century. The emergence of a creole preponderance marked the great ideological divide in the history of the slave revolts and undermined their restorationist quality. Creole-African unity made possible the great risings in

British Guiana, and in other cases, notably in Jamaica in 1831, the creoles either rose alone or at the leadership of a larger movement. In 1776 the Jamaican authorities reported creoles at the heart of a dangerous insurrectionary plot. The most ominous feature of this and other reports in the British Colonial Office files specified that the rebels were closely following the revolutionary developments in British North America.

After Jamaica exploded in 1831, Viscount Goderich reflected on the great change in a communication to the Earl of Belmore. So long as the slave trade had remained open, he began, Africans had predominated in Jamaica, and relations had remained stable. Viscount Goderich's reading of the tumultuous eighteenth-century record can hardly be accepted, but his comment on the new situation deserves respect. Now, he added, "an indigenous race of men has grown up, speaking our own language and instructed in our religion." Blind submission, he concluded, could no longer be expected. The Viscount had grasped, notwithstanding his misreading or misrepresentation of the African record, that the creoles, once drawn into the antislavery struggle, would bring with them an ideological perspective consistent with the political realities of the modern world. The Africans had raised formidable rebellions; the creoles were threatening revolution.

The Christmas rising on Jamaica in 1831 laid bare the new quality of the nineteenth-century slave revolts. The movement consisted of a number of isolated risings, at the heart of which about 150 slaves with about fifty guns organized a "black regiment" and fought hard; other actions came closer to qualifying as strikes, with or without a big dose of arson.

Large numbers of Jamaican slaves participated in some of its activity even if not the most militant or dramatic. The setting contained familiar elements. Blacks outnumbered whites about ten to one; the island had a tradition of revolt and maroon war; the planters were fighting a desperate battle against abolitionists in England; and the slaves threw up leaders from their most privileged strata.

The dissenting sects, long opposed by the slaveholders, had made considerable progress among the slaves and had attracted the support of abolitionists and reformers in England. The slaves retained much of their folk religion but increasingly blended into Baptist and Methodist beliefs and practices, as the white ministers strove to convert them. The missionaries did not counsel rebellion or disobedience but did preach a vigorous doctrine of spiritual equality, which the slaves translated into political terms. The rising came in the western parishes, which had had the greatest religious ferment. The political excitement occasioned by the spring abolitionist campaign in the House of Commons and the panic it inspired among white Jamaicans convinced the slaves that their masters were conspiring to thwart an imminent emancipation. The slaves were not far wrong. White Jamaicans in fact were debating resistance to the Crown, alliance with the United States, and other desperate measures. Before long, the literate slave leaders got a hearing for their claims that the masters were suppressing a decree of emancipation and plotting treason to the Crown.

The leadership of the revolt revealed the extent to which the slaves' movement for freedom was undergoing a radical transformation. Mary (Reckord) Turner, the foremost modern historian of the revolt, writes:

Out of this political ferment emerged leaders who directed the widespread excitement and discontent into action, utilizing religious meetings and the authority of the missionaries to promote the cause of freedom. The most outstanding rebel leader was Sam Sharpe, a domestic slave who worked in Montego Bay and was a member of the Baptist church there. Sharpe was literate, intelligent and ambitious and, like many of his kind, he found an outlet and a stimulant for his ambition in a mission church. As a convert, he displayed a talent for eloquent and passionate preaching which won him a position as leader, entrusted with the spiritual care of a class of other converts. Sharpe, however, was not content to serve simply within the church; he built up an independent connection with the "native" Baptists among whom he figured as a "daddy" or "ruler." At the same time he found mission teaching on obedience unsatisfactory. From his own reading of the Bible he became convinced that the slaves were entitled to freedom. This conviction, combined with the development of the emancipation campaign in England, of which Sharpe kept himself well informed, led him to believe that the slaves must make a bid for freedom. In recruiting aides, Sharpe naturally turned to other Baptist slaves.

The inspiration and organization for the revolt, therefore, came from the missions, although the white missionaries never intended their teachings and facilities to support violence. The slaves took up the Christian message, blended it with their traditional religion, and forged a moral case for action on behalf of their own freedom. But the revolt did not raise millennialist slogans or take on the features of a holy war. It applied religious sanction to a political demand for freedom. It neither continued the restorationist ideology of the earlier ethnic rebellions nor took utopian ground; it called for an end to slavery and, in effect, the extension of English liberties to the mass of the people. The origins of the revolt in the missions and its ideological connections with British abolitionism may help to account for its departure from the Jacobinism of the Haitian Revolution, which by 1831 had, in any case, spent its force. Thus, in its own way, the revolt of 1831 reflected the new forces that had been building since the American and French Revolutions had secularized the cause of national-popular liberation and proclaimed the Rights of Man.

The repressive measures that followed all the slave revolts, restorationist or modern, flowed from the exigencies of ruling-class power when confronted by opposition within and without. The consistently cruel nature of that repression, however, requires elaboration. After every slave revolt the whites cried out against the "barbarities," "cruelties," and "outrages" of the rebels and proceeded indiscriminately to slaughter countless innocent blacks. Violations of white womanhood caused particular concern. During the investigation of the Vesey plot much commotion surrounded the remark attributed to a single rebel leader that the slaves would know what to do with the white women. And much was made of the evidence that enraged slave rebels in Saint-Domingue had raped many white women, sometimes over the dead or dying bodies of their husbands. The fact remains: In the slave revolts of the hemisphere as a whole, rape occurred rarely despite the blacks' having had extreme provocation in the constant violation of their own women by whites. Neither Herbert Aptheker, who first challenged the conventional wisdom, nor anyone else has found evidence of a single rape during the revolts in the United States. During the long wave of slave revolts in Bahia (1807–1835), according to Howard Prince, only one case of rape has been documented.

The charge of slave barbarism during revolts rested on one point: the rebels had the audacity to kill whites, and even, as during the Nat Turner revolt, did not spare women and children. Since the first rule of such desperate warfare is to proceed as rapidly as possible before the more powerful enemy can regroup, compassion for women and children equaled a death warrant for the compassionate. That "bloodthirsty" Nat Turner ruined himself not by his executions but precisely by such compassion. Sheer bloodthirstiness by black rebels appeared during the revolts but neither often nor on a mass scale. The rebels in Bahia, for example, killed white soldiers but committed few if any atrocities against civilians. And as for that much-touted massacre of whites in Saint-Domingue, which occurred after the victory of the revolution, English agents deliberately urged it upon Dessalines against the wishes of his black generals. The English, knowing that Haiti was in desperate straits, offered trade and support in return for the extermination of their French rivals.

The slaveholders expressed unfeigned horror at the violence of the rebels and took appropriate measures to teach the savages a lesson. They responded as all ruling classes do when reminded that they too are mortal. The story is old and monotonous. Did the Central European peasants rise against their lords during the Reformation? The Hungarian serfs, among others, needed a lesson: seventy thousand would be slaughtered, with the leaders roasted over slow fires while their followers were forced to eat their flesh. (Whites, like blacks, have rarely hesitated to inflict the most grisly cruelties on their own people when property and class power have been at stake.) Did the Jacobins kill thousands of opponents during the Terror? The counterrevolutionary terror, which has not even earned a capital T in the literature, would kill many, many more. In the United States during the slave period, John Brown and his guerrillas struck terror into Virginians at Harpers Ferry and threatened to shed blood. Never mind that even in Kansas Brown's indefensible butchery had been politically selective and that he treated his prisoners in Virginia with exemplary restraint. Clearly, such murderous madmen deserved the worst, and the civilized citizens they were threatening were justified in shooting down Brown's emissaries despite their white flag; in mutilating his fallen warriors; and in lynching prisoners. Cynics might conclude that the moral of these stories is that a revolutionary terror had better do its work thoroughly.

The slaveholders, shocked by the evidence that the slaves had killed a few whites—so few in fact in the United States that Nat Turner's fifty or so victims seemed beyond belief— or that they had had the audacity to contemplate doing so, responded by showing just how much more civilized they were than their degraded slaves. The slaveholders swung into action with every rumor or suspicion. They lynched, burned alive, tortured, and dismembered suspected slaves, many of whom they later admitted had been innocent. The slaveholders of Louisiana who in 1811 spiked rebel heads to decorate the river road from New Orleans to Major Andre's plantation had not unleashed some early frontier temper that later generations would repudiate. In 1856 the slaveholders of Tennessee repeated the performance with a slight variation: They carried the impaled heads in a parade. And, unlike the

Louisianians of 1811, they had not even confronted slaves in arms; their victims had only fallen under suspicion of insurrectionary design.

The behavior of whites toward blacks, slave and free, whom they suspected of insurrection wrote a sadistic chapter in the history of American law and order. If slaves did not suffer lynching as often as free blacks did in the New South, they did suffer terribly in the wake of insurrection scares. The barbarism of the eighteenth and early nineteenth centuries carried down to the end of the regime, with some conscience-stricken slaveholders themselves providing the evidence for the atrocities committed by their neighbors against slaves, most of whom probably could not have been convicted even in a slaveholders' court of law. As William H. Thomson of Hinds County, Mississippi, wrote in 1835 during an insurrection scare that resulted in the lynching of a number of blacks and a few whites who tried to protect them, "It promises to become a greater evil than that it was intended to correct. The regulators need regulating." Their northern counterparts behaved no differently. The authorities in New York executed eighteen slave rebels in 1712: They manacled one and starved him to death, broke another on the wheel, and burned three others at the stake. Six of the condemned committed suicide.

The slaveholders of the United States set no special records in violence: Slaveholders in other countries proved every bit as adept. Captain Stedman reported from Surinam, "In 1730, a most shocking, and barbarous execution of eleven of the unhappy negro captives was resolved upon, in the expectation that it might terrify their companions and induce them to submit." The whites hanged one black man on a gibbet by an iron hook stuck through his ribs. (Nat Turner: "Was not Christ crucified?") They burned two others alive— slowly; broke six women on the rack; and decapitated two girls. "Such was their resolution under the torture," Stedman added, "that they endured them without even uttering a sigh." The "inhuman massacre," as he called it, had an effect opposite to that which the whites intended: The Saramaka rebels promptly intensified their attacks on the plantations and, after two decades of bloody struggle, forced the regime to peace terms.

In Barbados in 1675 the insurrection never took place, having been aborted after the whites learned of it from a woman house slave. White justice by court-martial claimed thirty-five lives by execution, including six burned alive and eleven beheaded and dragged through the streets *pour encourager les autres*. Tony, one of the blacks sent to the stake, refused to indulge anything except a piece of political wisdom: "If you Roast me today, you cannot Roast me tomorrow." The slaves at Plantation Poelwyck killed their overseer in 1731 and played football with his head. The whites, utterly revolted, would teach their slaves to behave like civilized human beings: Among other niceties, they roasted the rebel leader over a slow fire. Savage that he was, he succumbed quietly, smoking a pipe. During the sixteenth century the Spanish, who also roasted slave rebels, added a special touch. They chained their prisoners and set wild dogs to devour them. These events had parallels everywhere and during every period that slavery existed.

The slaves, as Nat Turner's revolt demonstrated, could do their share of burning and killing, and we might rush to excuse them, as Colonel Higginson did, by saying, "If it be the normal tendency of bondage to produce saints like Uncle Tom, let us all offer ourselves at auction immediately. . . . The difference was that the one brutality [of the slaveholders] was that of a mighty state, and the other was only the retaliation of its victims." Or we could recall the words of Gwyn Williams, in *Artisans and Sans Culottes*, "It was in blood, terror, and total war that democracy and democrats entered European history." Or we could quote Bertolt Brecht's *To Posterity* to answer those who wring their hands at the alleged savagery of slave risings:

> For we knew only too well:
> Even hatred of squalor
> Makes the brow grow stern
> Even anger against injustice
> Makes the voice grow harsh. Alas, we
> Who wished to lay the foundations of kindness
> Could not ourselves be kind.

Yet, these explanations, excuses, or proud defenses are beside the point: Atrocities by rebellious slaves in the United States did not occur often. Rebels killed whites but rarely tortured or mutilated them. They rarely, that is, committed against whites the outrages that whites regularly committed against them. Elsewhere in the hemisphere, where maroon wars and large-scale rebellions encouraged harsh actions, reactions, and reprisals, the level of violence and atrocity rose. But everywhere the overwhelming burden of evidence convicts the slaveholding regimes of countless crimes, including the most sadistic tortures, to every single act of barbarism by the slaves. C. L. R. James, whose history of the revolution in

Saint-Domingue scorns to minimize or apologize for the unseemly side of revolutionary violence, justly concludes his discussion of the rape and pillage committed by the slaves.

And yet they were surprisingly moderate, then and afterwards, far more humane than their masters had been or would ever be to them. They did not maintain this revengeful spirit for long. The cruelties of property and privilege are always more ferocious than the revenges of poverty and oppression. For the one aims at perpetuating resented injustice, the other is merely a momentary passion soon appeased.

With whatever degree of violence, Afro-American slave revolts affected the course of world history from the first and, in particular, contributed significantly to the shaping of the Age of Revolution. But did the slave revolts, like the great peasant wars, actually contribute much to the course of freedom?

The great historian and antifascist martyr Marc Bloch wrote in *French Rural History*:

Almost invariably doomed to defeat and eventual massacre the great [peasant] insurrections were altogether too disorganized to achieve any lasting result. The patient, silent struggles stubbornly carried on by rural communities over the years would accomplish more than these flashes in the pan. (p. 170)

That these patient, silent struggles, heroic enough in their own way, contributed immeasurably to the liberation of the peasantry ought not to be denied, and much the same could be said about those of the slaves of the United States who had little chance to take the revolutionary path. Without peasant and slave risings, however, the room for creative, peaceful effort would have shrunk considerably and might have disappeared.

The long-term results of popular risings, whether considered singly or in groups, will remain hotly debated, if for no other reason than that their evaluation ultimately rests upon the theoretical framework within which each historian, consciously or mindlessly, interprets historical process as a whole. Even for the short term, however, Bloch's remarks cannot stand empirical test. The contrary holds true, at least for some cases—which suffice to demonstrate that such rebellions could have salutary effect. Thus, the peasant risings in eastern Europe during the eighteenth and nineteenth centuries drove the ruling classes into compromise and reform. Thus, the Captain Swing movement in England impressed the landlords less by its weakness than by its very existence and contributed to the subsequent many-sided national reform. Thus, the innumerable peasant revolts in Russia during 1822–1861 stirred the intelligentsia to a belated concern with oppression and underscored the lesson of the Crimean War—that social backwardness spelled national humiliation and defeat. And the list could be much extended.

Apart from such forms of black militancy and military action as manifested during the great American struggle of 1861–1865, the direct efficacy of slave insurrection appeared most forcibly in the successful maroon wars in the Caribbean and in the quasi-insurgent struggles of the slaves in the Danish West Indies and in Brazil during the abolition crises of 1848 and 1871–1889 respectively. Well before the emergence of abolitionism and the Age of Revolution, maroon wars and slave revolts inhibited, if modestly, the expansion and consolidation of slavery. "The heavy expense of the 'maroon hunt,' following a slave rebellion," writes Gordon K. Lewis, "could cripple such vulnerable economies, as, indeed, St. John reverted to 'bush' for a generation after the ordeal of 1733." And during the wave of slave revolts that shook the British Caribbean during the 1730s and 1760s, there was, according to David Brion Davis, a direct correspondence between slave violence and the number of publications dealing with the problem of slavery in the colonies. Under the shock of the revolution in Saint-Domingue, the inhibition grew much more pronounced. The British decision to restrict the expansion of slavery in its newly acquired colonies of Trinidad and Guiana provides direct confirmation.

Slave revolts had a contradictory impact on the movement to ameliorate the rigors of slave life and upon the progress of Anglo-American abolitionism. The revolts often generated short-term reaction, with fearful immediate consequences for the slaves and additional difficulties for the abolitionists. For example, most Caribbean slave revolts stimulated British fears of social disorder and colonial race war and thereby inhibited the parliamentary maneuvering of those in England who were seeking to outlaw the Atlantic slave trade and ultimately to emancipate the slaves. Yet, in the specific political climate of 1831 the massive slave revolt in Jamaica—or the ghastly reprisals it provoked—played into abolitionist hands and contributed toward their triumph in 1833. And in the United States, as C. L. R. James has noted, Nat Turner made Garrison a household word. Notwithstanding the lack of formal connection between the two, white southerners seized upon Turner's revolt to suppress distribution of the *Liberator* and put a price on Garrison's head.

The influence of the slave revolts on the condition of the

slaves also followed a contradictory course. Gabriel Prosser, Denmark Vesey, and Nat Turner provoked waves of repression: restrictions on literacy, preaching, manumission, and much else. But they also made the slaveholders thoughtful and encouraged those who argued that the best antidote to rebellion was better food, clothing, and shelter, more leisure time, and firmer measures against brutality. The two tendencies went hand-in-hand. While taking measures to confirm the blacks in perpetual slave status and to reduce their room for political initiatives, the southern slaveholders tried to make slavery itself a more bearable condition. The period from Nat Turner to secession unfolded as a great reaction and, simultaneously, as a modest tempering of the day-to-day rigors of the system.

On balance, the revolts made a substantial contribution to the amelioration of the material conditions of slave life, for they provided one of the major spurs to the abolition of the African slave trade. In the United States, especially, the closing of the trade, with its attendant rise in the price of labor, compelled the slaveholders to adopt measures designed to guarantee the productivity and reproduction of their labor force.

W. E. B. Du Bois, writing at the end of the nineteenth century, drew attention to the significance of slave revolt for the abolition of the slave trade. The slaveholders, he argued, recognized the increase of blacks relative to whites and of Africans relative to creoles as a harbinger of new and greater risings. Recent scholarship has introduced important qualifications into this thesis but basically has sustained it. The earliest measures to restrict the trade to South Carolina, for example, originated in the wake of the Stono Rebellion and the decisive state measures of the 1790s, which paved the way for the national prohibition of 1808, reflected nothing so much as the fear of another Saint-Domingue. True, other forces intervened, and the fear of revolt might not have sufficed. But few if any great political changes occur in response to a single pressure, and the discovery of a conjuncture of forces does not negate Du Bois's insight. South Carolina's decision in 1787 to suspend the trade for three years had much to do with the rivalry of the up country with the low country and with the interest of the big rice planters in driving up slave prices. But, after the trade reopened, the willingness of the slaveholders to swallow federal abolition undoubtedly flowed in part from their reflections on Saint-Domingue and on such warnings as those sent by Gabriel Prosser and the widespread conspiracy of 1802. And in colonial Louisiana, as James McGowan has shown, the combination of black resistance with a labor shortage forced a normally intransigent slaveholding class to institute reforms, including those designed to protect black family life.

Had the slaveholders' fear of slave revolt produced only the abolition of the Atlantic trade, the victory might have been theirs, born of fear or no, for the amelioration in the material conditions of slave life advanced in step with the confirmation of slave status and the heightening of the psychological ravages of racism. But that fear had additional consequences, which indirectly strengthened the slaves' confidence in ultimate deliverance. The defense of the southern social order increasingly required the suppression of elementary civil liberties not only in the South but throughout the United States. The famous "gag rule" in Congress, the tampering with the mails, the shrill demands for the suppression of free speech and assembly for abolitionists, and the contempt for home rule implicit in the Fugitive Slave Law's administrative provisions did for the enemies of slavery what they could not easily have done for themselves: They associated slavery with an arrogant and reactionary social class prepared to trample on the time-honored and blood-won rights of white Americans. The abolitionists might have shouted forever that the black man too had rights. The pervasive racism of the North promised little or no response. But the abolitionists said more. They insisted that the suppression of the rights of black people spelled the suppression of the rights of white people. Only the slaveholders by their ever-increasing and unavoidable recklessness could demonstrate the deadly truth of this charge.

The slaveholders had no choice except to increase the political stakes, for they understood that their safety required maximum protection. It is pointless to argue that they exaggerated the danger of slave revolt and to dwell on the infrequency and low intensity of actual revolt. The slaveholders sensibly believed that revolt would occur much more frequently and with greater intensity if the balance of power were altered. And any fool could see that the dissemination of abolitionist pamphlets would expose the growing moral and political isolation of the slave regime in the country and the world and would eventually affect that balance. Even the southern Unionists had to temper their attacks on nullification and extremism so as not to provoke slave disorder. They thereby weakened their own political position and inadvertently reinforced the growing feeling that the South was becoming a monolithic and reactionary society. For the slave-holders, even more readily than for others, the price of liberty —their own—was eternal vigilance.

Yes, the slave revolts in the South did not rival in frequency and intensity those of Jamaica, the Guianas, or Brazil, not to mention Saint-Domingue. But, if the slaves had not risen at Stono, in southern Louisiana, in Southampton County, if they had not come close to rising in Richmond and in Charleston, if they had not risen at all, would the sober, martial, experienced political leaders of the slaveholding class have risked a dangerous confrontation with the North, including their own traditional northern political allies, simply because they were hearing horror stories from other slave countries? Why should they have? They considered themselves the guardians of the most humane, materially comfortable, and militarily stable slave regime in history. But despite all the cant about having loyal, contented, faithful slaves, they could not escape the recognition that a Nat Turner might appear anywhere at any time. During Virginia's great debate over emancipation, conducted in the wake of Nat Turner's revolt, James McDowell taunted the proslavery spokesmen:

> Was it the fear of Nat Turner, and his deluded, drunken handful of followers, which produced such effects? . . . No sir: it was the suspicion eternally attached to the slave himself—the suspicion that a Nat Turner might be in every family; that the same bloody deed might be acted over at any time and in any place; that the materials for it were spread through the land, and were always ready for a like explosion. Nothing but the force of this withering apprehension . . . could have thrown a brave people into consternation, or

116

could have made any portion of this powerful Commonwealth, for a single instant, to have quailed and trembled.

McDowell had a long line of predecessors throughout the hemisphere. Recall, for example, the words of John Vaughton, manager of the Codrington estate in Barbados in 1738: "That is what Every Person who are Dwellers here knows, that the best of them are at All times ready to joyn in A Conspiracy . . . Against the best of Masters and Overseers."

That recognition, even as expressed in Vaughton's exaggerated way, stemmed precisely from actual experience with slave revolts, however limited, including abortive revolts and plots. As James Hugo Johnston has written in *Race Relations in Virginia and Miscegenation in the South*:

> The faithful slave gained respect and sympathy for his fellows, but the rebellious spirit created grave fears that bloodshed and suffering would be inflicted on the South if the Negroes were forced to remain forever in bondage. The spirit of rebellion taught many citizens that there were slaves who wanted to be free. Had all the slaves been docile and content, it might have been possible to hold the Negro as a slave indefinitely, but the violent spirits made the slave system a problem that would not be silenced.

Those revolts and the fear they inspired drove the slaveholders into a fateful constitutional and political confrontation with northerners who cared little or nothing about the oppression of black people—a confrontation that ended with the destruction of the slaveholders' regime.

Both directly and through intersection with wider movements of national liberation, the slave revolts formed a vital part of the international revolutionary tidal wave that brought the modern world to fruition. Paradoxically, the revolts helped, as did other radical popular movements, to assure the international consolidation and expansion of Anglo-American capitalism both politically, in the influence on a new balance of world power, and ideologically, in their strengthening of the bourgeois idea of property. Yet, being mass movements of the nonwhite laboring poor, they also challenged, if often only implicitly, the new forms of exploitation and oppression inherent in the triumphant capitalist world-system. Normally, the slave revolts resembled worldwide peasant revolts in at least one decisive respect: If successful, they necessarily fell under the sway of more advanced social classes. Peasants have nowhere been able to create a state of their own, for their form of property cannot sustain one; they ultimately have had to support a state that, however powerful in itself, primarily serves the interests of a class capable of organizing the social and productive system. In modern times this process has generally served the interests of the bourgeoisie, whatever concessions it has had to make to those who directly control the state or to the peasants themselves. During the twentieth century Lenin, Mao, Ho, and others have demonstrated that peasant wars may be put to other uses.

Afro-American slaves, unlike most peasants and unlike the slaves of the ancient world, consciously willed their own elimination as a class and consciously sought to rebuild society on a new property base. The restorationist maroons worked out their own solution, which ended in their tangential relationship to the mainstream of historical development. The breakthrough came with the essentially bourgeois-democratic revolution in Saint-Domingue, which conceded land and a measure of security to the ex-slaves—to, in Sidney Mintz's suggestive phrase, "the reconstituted peasantry." That the revolution ended in the triumph of a comprador bourgeoisie and a parasitic state merely provides a special case of the general rule. Everywhere else the slave revolts merged with larger struggles for national liberation and sociopolitical reform and benefited the bourgeoisie while encouraging the masses to challenge racism, exploitation, and oppression. Despite the counterrevolutionary outcome, these harsh battles enabled the masses to glimpse their long-term strength and to prepare themselves, however haltingly, for the many struggles ahead.

Slave revolts and other forms of violent resistance during the Age of Revolution shaped and were shaped by those struggles for national liberation and social change too often presented as the work of lily-white elites. During the South American wars of independence, both loyalists and revolutionaries followed an uncertain course in relation to blacks in general and slaves in particular. Both had a stake in the suppression of the social question, and both had a vested interest in slave property. Yet, the exigencies of protracted war led each not only to enlist black troops with promises of emancipation but to encourage slave rebellion behind the other's lines.

When the national-liberation movements faltered in their sometime commitment to emancipation, the blacks shifted to the royalist side, as, for example, when armed slaves helped to crush the first Venezuelan Republic; and in numerous instances they rose against one or another side to defend their rights and realize their aspirations in what a Spanish official wryly termed *"insurrección de otra especie."* If nothing else, these risings destroyed the myth of slave docility and contentment and taught the leaders of both sides that whoever won would have a formidable "black problem" on his hands. Black militancy helped push the wavering Bolívar into his famous alliance with Haiti's Pétion and into bolder efforts toward emancipation. Developments in Venezuela, in turn, generated the first great black conspiracy in Puerto Rican history. Despite the vicissitudes of abolition politics during the next few decades in South America, the widespread enlistment of black troops, the slave risings, and the developing self-confidence of the black communities helped put one new republic after another on the road to emancipation.

The national revolutions, with their heightened sensitivity to questions of "freedom," "autonomy," and even "equality," generated a crisis of conscience over slavery itself. Logic and revolutionary idealism demanded the repudiation of slavery as a matter of principle and, unlike the United States and Brazil, the new nations of Spanish America did not contain slaveholding classes powerful enough to dominate society. Final emancipation took a long time, but the end was in sight with the dawn of national independence. The national revolutions, spurred by the action of armed blacks either in revolt or in republican uniform, undermined the slave regimes in Spanish-speaking South and Central America and reduced the slaveholding region to the Old South, the Caribbean, and Brazil. British emancipation in 1833, which followed the completion of the wars of national liberation, hastened the final settlement of the slavery question in South America and threw the remaining slaveholding classes irrevocably on the defensive.

The revolutionary year 1848 marked the end of slavery in

the Danish and French islands, although not without massive action by the slaves in their own behalf. The American and Brazilian slaveholders, now almost completely isolated, could take little comfort from their politically weak Cuban and Dutch Caribbean counterparts, who in time would recapitulate the South American and Danish experiences. The "course of the South to secession"—to recall Phillips' phrase —and the ultimate destruction of New World slavery had been powerfully accelerated by Spanish-speaking whites, browns, and blacks, however tenuous and episodic their alliance in a seemingly remote and tangential struggle, the significance of which seemed so much less than that of such American textbook events as the battle of New Orleans, the panic of 1819, or the Missouri Compromise.

The post-restorationist slave revolts, beginning with the revolution in Saint-Domingue, imposed themselves on world history as a vital part of the bourgeois-democratic and national-liberation process begun in the English colonies of North America and brought to fierce climax in France. Among the central features of the revolutionary epoch was the dramatic forward movement of the masses on the terrain of secular policies and ideology. Eric Hobsbawm writes in *Primitive Rebels*:

> The American and French Revolutions of the eighteenth century are probably the first mass political movements in the history of the world which expressed their ideology and aspirations in terms of secular rationalism and not of traditional religion. The fact marks a revolution in the life and thought of the common people so profound that its nature is difficult even to appreciate for those of us who have grown up in an epoch when politics is agnostic.

Secularization democratized revolutionary ideology and prepared the common people for a more autonomous role in revolutionary struggle. True, modern revolutionary political parties and movements have retained many important features of militant millenarianism, including projections of human perfection and a secularized version of the Kingdom of God on Earth; a tendency to resurrect the Manichaean struggle of Christ against Antichrist so recurrent in radical Christian heresies; the cult of the infallible leader; and that certainty of deliverance which has paradoxically often proven necessary to stimulate revolutionary voluntarism. This familiar criticism, repeated ad nauseam by those who would denigrate modern revolutionary movements by linking them with irrationalism and fanaticism, does demonstrate the power of cultural inheritance and even sheds light on the psychological dimension of historical process. It remains, nonetheless, radically false.

Modern revolutionary movements, beginning with the moderate ideology of the leaders of the American Revolution and especially with Jacobinism in both its French and Haitian forms, took a new turn, notwithstanding the substantial measure of historical continuity they represented. They introduced considerable rationalism into older ideas and projected a more realistic view of human nature and action. Specifically, their break with the ideas of supernatural deliverance enormously reinforced the demand for the assertion of human will and significantly reduced, although they did not eliminate, the tendency toward Manichaean fanaticism. Such movements have thrown up messiahs and sometimes almost deified them, but they have generally responded to charismatic leaders with a degree of realism and restraint hardly possible for those following a prophet and a revelation. This shift, however partial, away from the tradition of revolutionary millenarianism has created unprecedented room for autonomous popular action; it has, in fact, required that action even while creating new methods of restraint and repression. The significance, for example, of the gradual transfer of allegiance from the prophetic leader to the party, the movement, or the nation has narrowed the possibilities for acquiring blind loyalty. And for these very reasons the secularization of revolutionary ideology has vastly improved the chance of victory. Stripped of the requirements of prophetic specificity and of the myth of the divinely chosen leader, the party can much more readily prepare the masses for tactical retreats and compromises and for the acceptance of defeat and even disaster while it regroups in protracted war.

Toussaint's suppression of Vodûn, his attempt at state control of Roman Catholicism, and his own brand of Jacobinism provided a powerful example of this new stage, which had been prefigured in the political thought of Machiavelli and which, despite its cynical aspect, expressed the need to ground a basically secular ideology in a doctrine of moral obligation. Toussaint's course provided an illustration of Hobsbawm's trenchant observation in *The Age of Revolution*: "This secularism of the revolution demonstrates the remarkable political hegemony of the liberal middle class, which imposed its political ideological forms on a much vaster movement of the masses."

The revolution in Saint-Domingue marked the passage from an Afro-American religious call to holy war to the universalist claims of the Rights of Man. Stage one: the Vodûn high priest Boukman tells his followers to discard their crucifixes and to prepare for war against the infidels: "Throw away the Symbol of the god of the whites who has often caused us to weep, and listen to the voice of liberty, which speaks in the hearts of us all." Stage two: In 1792 the black revolutionary leaders Jean-François and Biassou, wishing to negotiate a compromise, heatedly reply to French demands that they disband their army as the price for peace:

> How can we accept your demand to "go home"? One hundred thousand men are in arms. We are dependent upon the general will—and what a general will! That of a multitude of negroes from the African coast, who for the most part do not know two words of French, yet who have been warriors in their own country.

Stage three: Toussaint assumes leadership of the revolution, allies with the Jacobins, and eventually issues his own constitution, which confirms these "Coast Negroes" who "do not know two words of French" in their new, hard-won status, defined by the constitution as "free and French."

Toussaint's determination to link an independent black Saint-Domingue with revolutionary France reflected his deep grasp of the political and economic realities of the modern world. His new state would be independent and autonomous in virtual dominion status within the orbit of revolutionary France. And while his astute foreign policy placed national security above ideology and exhibited startling zig-zags, which critics have denounced as lack of principle, Toussaint dreamed of someday leading an invasion of Africa to destroy the slave trade and to build an empire of his own, apparently so that Africans, too, might be "free and French."

Toussaint understood his revolution's international context, for, as Hobsbawm adds, "All plans of European liberation until 1848 hinged on a joint rising of peoples under the leadership of the French to overthrow European reaction." The prestige of the great French revolution and the military state power to which it gave rise guaranteed French hegemony over revolutionaries in Europe and the Americas, much as during the twentieth century the prestige of the Russian Revolution and its subsequent consolidation of state power long guaranteed the hegemony of the Stalinist Third International over revolutionaries throughout the world. In time the reactionary features of the socially contradictory Bonapartist expansion would reinforce the growing sense among American and European revolutionaries that neither God nor the French would save them and that they would have to look elsewhere, especially to themselves, for inspiration and material power. But for a prolonged period the black struggle for freedom pushed forward within an international bourgeois-democratic mainstream.

"The Flag of *Our* Country"

What did ignorant field hands in Virginia or South Carolina know or care about the ideals of the American and French Revolutions and of the Declarations of Independence and of the Rights of Man? C. L. R. James, who pioneered in treating the slave revolts as part of the international bourgeois-democratic revolutionary movements, forcefully replied that the slaves of Saint-Domingue and the *sans culottes* of Paris together radicalized the French Revolution by projecting a political vision much more democratic than the republicanism being advanced by the liberal bourgeoisie. W. E. B. Du Bois provided a complementary answer: "There are today no truer exponents of the pure human spirit of the Declaration of Independence than the American Negroes."

However much some might wish to dismiss these claims as romantic exaggeration, the slaveholders knew better. The southern Federalists, for example, berated the Jeffersonians for spreading a French gospel of liberty, equality, and fraternity that the slaves would hear, interpret with deadly literalness, and rally around. Increasingly, during the nineteenth century, slaveholders lectured each other on the need to keep the blacks away from Fourth of July orations. The Reverend C. F. Sturgis of South Carolina left us a memorable image of

the Fourth as a plantation holiday, at least as seen through the
masters' eyes:

> Sheep and pigs and other fatlings are killed and a beautiful,
> though not very *magnificent* dinner is provided. Master and
> mistress and neighbors, and negroes assemble, and black and
> white are seen strung along a great table, like the keys of a
> piano; and like the aforesaid instrument, the black keys make
> fully as much noise as the white; all mingle for awhile in the
> utmost harmony and good feeling; many a merry joke goes
> round, songs are sung, and all is rustic hilarity and mirth.
> . . . [But these celebrations must be] strictly a *negro* and
> *family* affair, and the negroes themselves should be their own
> orators, actors, and *musicians*. Instead of singing "Hail Co-
> lumbia," let them sing "Walk-jaw-bone"; instead of march-
> ing to the strains of martial music, let them engage in the
> more congenial employment of patting "Juber," and instead
> of listening to the rehearsal of the victories over the British,
> let them rejoice in their well-earned triumph in their long,
> hard contest with "General Green" that is with crab-grass.
> . . . Their weak minds are liable to be led astray—the plain-
> est things are likely to be perverted or exaggerated.

The Reverend Mr. Sturgis had his problems, for the
Fourth remained the Fourth, and the slaveholders could not
always keep their slaves isolated at politically innocuous lay-
by barbecues. The slaves loved to see and hear the white politicians put-on-dog, and many masters thought their slaves
too stupid to reflect on what they heard. As late as 1825 an
orator at a big fête caused trouble by toasting, "Freedom to
the slave," but thereafter the speeches became safe enough.
By the 1840s the orators might even roast the abolitionists.
Forgetting the early warnings of the southern Federalists,

they continued to sound themes acceptable to southern white opinion and ostensibly irrelevant to the slaves, for whom the cheers for Brazilian, Greek, or Hungarian freedom supposedly could mean nothing. Nor, apparently, could the loose talk about "independence," "war against tyrants," "right of revolution," or, for that matter, "southern rights."

Harriet Martineau, in *Retrospect of Western Travel*, told the story of a slave in Massachusetts who heard of the Bill of Rights and demanded her freedom. Asked how she had heard of such things, she gave an answer that might easily have come from anywhere in the South: "By keepin' still and mindin' things." Some ex-slaves interviewed during the twentieth century recalled the Fourth of July as a big holiday but added that they heard no political speeches. Many others did report having heard them, as worried slavery stalwarts constantly insisted. And even with maximum security and major efforts to keep the slaves away from political meetings, the danger remained. The Fourth was a major plantation holiday with much coming and going by black friends from other plantations. House slaves and field hands mingled in easy camaraderie at generous barbecues. Some house slaves attended their masters at political meetings, even if the slaves were generally excluded, and they reported back what they saw and heard.

Every election campaign echoed the language of the American Revolution and threatened to generate slave unrest no matter how much care was taken to control the rhetoric. In 1840, for example, a slaveholder ordered Tom, his slave, to do a job and got a sharp refusal: "Please de Lord, old Tip's elected, and I a free man." On February 22, 1849, the *Plant-*

ers' Banner of St. Mary's Parish, Louisiana, explained the incident under the title "A Wrong Impression":

> The tendency of the habit of Southern politicians representing Northern Presidential candidates as Abolitionists is laughably illustrated by the following anecdote, told by Dr. Elder. The Democratic stumpers, during the Presidential campaign of 1840, were in the habit of charging General Harrison with Abolitionism; the slaves everywhere heard it, and when the news of his election reached them, the poor creatures thought their time had come at last.

The great wave of slave unrest that so frightened the white South in 1856 came in the wake of the Republican party's emergence and fierce campaign. The bloodbath in Tennessee, in which alleged slave conspirators met a ghastly fate, may in fact have been linked to a widespread plot throughout the western slave states, as some historians believe, but evidence remains scarce. Benjamin F. Allen of Tennessee wrote to William Trousdale on January 8, 1857, that white southerners believed in such a plot, and he attributed the hanging of four blacks in Gallatin to a growing panic. He added, "The whole thing was greatly exaggerated and no doubt had its origins in the late Presidential canvass, the negroes hearing so much of Fremont began to think that if he was elected that they would all be free, but I have no idea that there was any organized plan for insurrection."

Several insurrectionary plots projected the Fourth of July as the day to rise—for example, the aborted but impressive plot at Camden, South Carolina, in 1816. Since the whites would leave their plantations to attend rallies and barbecues with flowing liquor, the decision had a simple practical purpose, but it also had a powerful symbolic meaning. The slaves displayed too great a poetic sense to permit a narrow reading of their intentions. And was it coincidence that Denmark Vesey, who so long brooded over the meaning of Haiti, originally chose Bastille Day as the day on which his great insurrection would begin?

The slaves' Christianity sang of freedom and deliverance and blended easily into the political message of the Revolutionary War. The religion of the slaves, at least during the nineteenth century, normally eschewed calls to insurrection and took the path of long-term survival in a world of hopeless odds, but its essentially militant core could be turned into revolutionary channels at given moments. Thus, the message of the Revolution, in the hands of a Gabriel Prosser, a Denmark Vesey, or a Nat Turner, could be made to reinforce rather than challenge the religious spirit of the people. The slaves had been promised deliverance by Moses, who, transformed into Jesus, had offered individual salvation in the next world while maintaining the promise of collective emancipation in this world in God's good time. For the slaves the freedom and equality proclaimed by the Revolutionary generation represented a step in the unfolding of His will, not merely for themselves but for everyman, as such spirituals as "Didn't My Lord Deliver Daniel" so eloquently demonstrate. Thus, the Reverend C. C. Jones warned his fellow slaveholders to grasp the meaning of the Camden plot of 1816. The leaders, in his partisan view, were not really Christians at all. They were, he charged, invoking the words of E. C. Holland, fanatics imbued "by wild and frantic ideas of the rights of man, *and the misconstrued injunctions and examples of Holy Writ!*" In the 1850s the slaveholders tried to be more careful, and the slaves heard fewer inflammatory speeches. Fewer—but still too many.

The attitudes of northern free blacks, especially those active in the abolitionist movement, reflected a deep ambivalence toward the Fourth of July, often misrepresented for modern political purposes. The speeches and writings of these leaders, some of them ex-slaves, increasingly dwelt on the blatant contradiction between the sentiments of the Declaration of Independence and the continued existence of slavery and extreme racial discrimination. They mercilessly exposed the shallowness of white pretensions and held up the Constitution as well as the Declaration as evidence of white hypocrisy. The Fourth of July increasingly evoked bitterness and contempt from northern black communities, which preferred to celebrate the day of British Emancipation or no day at all.

To a large extent black spokesmen assaulted the slaveholders and their northern protectors by the simple but powerful device of holding up a mirror and bearing witness to the reflected image. No one did so with such dramatic effect as Frederick Douglass in his great speech on "The Meaning of the Fourth of July for the Negro," delivered in Rochester, New York, in 1852.

Douglass had more than once told whites that no self-respecting black could love or consider as home a country that enslaved his brothers and sisters. He repeatedly referred to the Fourth and to American institutions and traditions as "yours." The Fourth, he began his speech in Rochester, "is the birthday of your national independence, and of your political freedom." And he probably intended the biting irony with which he invoked the biblical exodus so important to

the imagery of the freedom-loving slaves: "This, to you, is
what the Passover was to the emancipated people of God."
The heart of his indictment deserves extensive quotation:

> Fellow citizens, pardon me, allow me to ask, why am I called
> upon to speak here today? What have I, or those I represent,
> to do with your national independence? Are the great prin-
> ciples of political freedom and of natural justice, embodied
> in that Declaration of Independence, extended to us? and am
> I, therefore, called upon to bring our humble offering to the
> national altar, and to confess the benefits and express devout
> gratitude for the blessings resulting from your independence
> to us? . . . Your high independence only reveals the im-
> measurable distance between us. The blessings in which you,
> this day, rejoice, are not enjoyed in common. The rich in-
> heritance of justice, liberty, prosperity and independence,
> bequeathed by your fathers, is shared by you, not by me. The
> sunlight that brought light and healing to you, has brought
> stripes and death to me. This Fourth of July is *yours*, not
> *mine. You* may rejoice *I* must mourn. . . . What, to the
> American slave, is your Fourth of July? I answer: a day that
> reveals to him, more than all other days in the year, the gross
> injustice and cruelty to which he is the constant victim. To
> him, your celebration is a sham; your boasted liberty an un-
> holy license; your national greatness swelling vanity; your
> sounds of rejoicing are empty and heartless; your denuncia-
> tion of tyrants brass-fronted impudence; your shouts of liber-
> ty and equality hollow mockery; your prayers and hymns,
> your sermons and thanksgivings, with all your religious pa-
> rade and solemnity, are to Him mere bombast, fraud, decep-
> tion, impiety and hypocrisy—a thin veil to cover up crimes
> which would disgrace a nation of savages. There is not a
> nation on the earth guilty of practices more shocking and
> bloody than are the people of the United States at this very
> hour.

Yet, Douglass said much more. Early in the speech he had noted:

> Fellow citizens, I am not wanting in respect for the fathers of this republic. The signers of the Declaration of Independence were brave men. They were great men, too—great enough to give frame to a great age. It does not often happen to a nation to raise, at one time, such a number of truly great men. The point from which I am compelled to view them is not, certainly, the most favorable; and yet I cannot contemplate their great deeds with less than admiration. They were statesmen, patriots and heroes, and for the good they did, and the principles they contended for, I will unite with you to honor their memory.

Toward the end he indignantly denounced the doctrine that the Constitution guaranteed and sanctioned slavery: "Interpreted as it ought to be interpreted, the Constitution is a glorious liberty document. Read its Preamble, consider its purposes." And he expressed hope for a country still young and capable of change in a world in which "there are forces in operation which must inevitably work the downfall of slavery . . . I, therefore, leave off where I began, with hope. While drawing encouragement from 'the Declaration of Independence,' the great principles it contains and the genius of American institutions, my spirit is cheered by the obvious tendencies of the age."

Douglass' words, in their attack on white hypocrisy and their unfeigned admiration for American political principles, reverberate through the writings and speeches of antebellum black Americans. Sterling Stuckey, in his admirable introduction to *Ideological Origins of Black Nationalism*, writes of even the militant forerunners of black nationalism, "There was no small admiration among distinguished blacks for America's 'free institutions,' even though there was intense hatred of slavery and oppression." The deep impression made by the great ideas of the Age of Revolution on black Americans, free and slave, might seem obvious and unworthy of extended comment, were it not that some historians, most notably Theodore Draper, have implausibly cited this deep impression as evidence for an alleged repudiation of black nationalism, or that embittered black nationalists, more plausibly but nonetheless tragically, have cited the critical attacks on the tradition of the Fourth as evidence of the opposite.

The great ideological advance of the Age of Revolution reflected the struggle of the slaves of the New World and the masses of the Old, notwithstanding their intellectual formulation by bourgeois revolutionaries who often preferred to give their own words a more restricted interpretation. The masses, black and white, heard and understood the words, which were clear enough, and put the "interpretation" down to greed, hypocrisy, and the spirit of Judas.

The question has little or nothing to do with separatism versus integrationism, for blacks of both persuasions cannot escape an inheritance common to all Americans. A separate nation-state formed by American blacks, were one to emerge, would inherit notions of freedom and democracy hammered out by blacks as well as whites during the Age of Revolution and magnificently expressed by the Founding Fathers, the Jacobins of Paris, and the revolutionary leaders of Saint-Domingue. And these notions have a particular context, which expresses much more than the longing of people everywhere to be free of oppressors. In this sense, the American Founding Fathers spoke for the deepest aspirations of black as

well as white America, however much they dishonored themselves by betraying some of their own highest principles.

Black Americans will decide for themselves the relative
merits of separatist and integrationist ideologies and strate-
gies, which in any case have rarely if ever been sustained in
absolute form. Whatever their ultimate decision, they share
with white Americans and certain other peoples affected by
the spirit and principles of the English, American, and
French Revolutions, a commitment to the reconciliation of
individual freedom with democracy—a precious commitment increasingly scarce on both sides of the cold war.

In no other terms can we make sense of the choice of those
antebellum blacks who spurned African colonization and yet
repudiated the United States to live in Canada or England,
or of those who worked for the creation of a great "Afro-
Saxon" empire in the Caribbean. Ignorant and illiterate as
the slaves generally were, they grasped the issue at least as
well as others, for their own history of struggle against enslavement in the world's greatest bourgeois democracy led
them to recognize and to seize upon the link between the
freedom of the individual proclaimed to the world by Christianity and the democratization of the bourgeois revolution,
which was transforming that fateful idea into a political reality. Not surprisingly, William Craft, in his preface to the
narrative of his and Ellen Craft's escape from slavery, cited
two ideas as having unfit them for slavery: the biblical assertion that God made all men of one blood; and the egalitarian
principles of the Declaration of Independence.

During the war, as the Union troops occupied more and
more southern territory, the blacks reversed the attitude of
their northern brothers and made the Fourth their own holi-

day, which it remained after the war. A special meaning attached to a little boy's reading the Declaration of Independence to the freemen of Port Royal, as did the action of a Baptist congregation on St. Helena, which rose, three hundred strong, to sing:

> Roll, Jordan, Roll, Jordan!
> Roll, Jordan, Roll.

Lucy McKim Garrison commented:

> It swelled forth like a triumphal anthem. That same hymn was sung by thousands of Negroes on the 4th of July last, when they marched in procession under the Stars and Stripes, cheering them for the first time as the "flag of *our* country." A friend writing from there says the chorus was indescribably grand—"that the whole woods and world seemed joining in that rolling sound."

What did the Fourth, the Declaration of Independence, and the "flag of *our* country" mean to those illiterate slaves and freedmen? Were the slaveholders right in sometimes asserting that their chattel heard nothing more than bombast, either rendered as meaningless excitement or unfortunate incitement to primitive assertion and license? Corporal Prince Lambkin provided an unforgettable answer. An ex-slave transformed into a tough soldier, he rose to speak to his fellow black troops in Colonel Higginson's regiment. He began by reminding them that he had predicted war ever since Fremont's campaign in 1856. And then, in those blunt accents which the people everywhere deserve to hear from their leaders but so rarely do, he combined in a single stroke the profound religious faith of his people with the political message they were ready to hear:

136

Our mas'rs dey hab lib under de flag, dey got dere wealth under it, and ebryting beautiful for dere chilen. Under it dey hab grind us up, and put us in dere pocket for money. But de fus' minute dey tink dat ole flag mean freedom for we colored people, dey pull it right down, and run up de rag ob dere own. [immense applause.] But we'll neber desert de ole flag, boys, neber; we hab lib under it for *eighteen hundred sixty-two years*, and we'll die for it now.

Bibliographical Essay

Since slave revolt did not occur in a vacuum, a full bibliography would have to include virtually everything on slavery itself. Thus, for the hemisphere as a whole one should begin with the larger surveys. Indispensable for the historical context of the revolts and of modern slavery generally are Eric Hobsbawm, *The Age of Revolution, 1789–1848* (New York, 1962); David Brion Davis, *The Problem of Slavery in Western Culture* (Ithaca, N.Y., 1966), and *The Problem of Slavery in the Age of Revolution* (Ithaca, N.Y., 1975). See also two valuable general works: C. Duncan Rice, *The Rise and Fall of Black Slavery* (New York, 1975); and Philip Foner, *History of Black Americans: From Africa to the Emergence of the Cotton Kingdom* (Westport, Conn., 1975). Roger Bastide offers controversial interpretations of maroon life and other subjects in *African Civilizations in the Americas* (New York, 1972). His views are effectively challenged at some points by Richard Price in his introduction to his splendid collection of studies, *Maroon Societies* (New York, 1973), which includes some illuminating contemporary materials, essays by leading scholars, and a fine bibliography. Sidney W. Mintz's important studies of maroon life and the role of the African peoples in the development of Caribbean societies have been collected in *Caribbean Transformations* (Chicago, 1974).

Any consideration of the revolts themselves should begin with C. L. R. James's great historical work and Marxist interpretation, *Black Jacobins: Toussaint L'Ouverture and the San Domingo Revolution* (New York, 1938). Less useful—one great book should be enough for a lifetime—but still worth reading are James, *A History of Negro Revolt* (New York, 1969), and "The Atlantic Slave Trade and Slavery: Some Interpretations of their Significance in the Development of the United States and the Western World," *Amistad*, No. 1 (New York, 1970), 119–64. A seminal interpretation of the slave revolts as part of the bourgeois-democratic era, with implications beyond that era, may be found in the voluminous work of W. E. B. Du Bois.

A wide-ranging collection of papers and commentaries on various aspects of slavery in the New World may be found in Vera Rubin and Arthur Tuden, eds., *Comparative Perspectives on Slavery in New World Plantation Societies*. Much of the material in this large (618 closely packed pages) book bears on our subject, but especially relevant is Part VI on resistance, which contains papers by Richard Frucht (St. Kitts); Mavis C. Campbell (Jamaica); Leslie F. Manigat (Saint-Domingue); Angelina Pollak-Eltz (Venezuela); Luz María Martínez Montiel (Mexico); Silvia de Groot (Surinam); Oruno D. Lara (comparative); and Michael (Gerald W.) Mullin (the United States; with commentaries by Herbert Aptheker and Richard Price.

For the hemispheric social context and for an introductory bibliography see Laura Foner and Eugene D. Genovese, eds., *Slavery in the New World* (Englewood Cliffs, N.J., 1969). For an early readable and instructive attempt to set the revolts in a hemispheric perspective see Thomas Wentworth Higginson, *Black Rebellion* (New York, 1969), originally written for *Atlantic Monthly* during the 1850s and 1860s and published as part of *Travellers and Outlaws* in 1889; also relevant is his better-known *Army Life in a Black Regiment* (Boston, 1870). Important general works with useful discussions of slave revolt include Sir Harry Johnston, *The Negro in the New World* (London, 1910); and Noel Deerr, *The History of Sugar* (2 vols.; London, 1945).

For slavery in the United States begin with the work of Ulrich Bonnell Phillips, which although deeply flawed by racist bias, remains indispensable: *American Negro Slavery* (Baton Rouge, 1967); *Life and Labor in the Old South* (Boston, 1948); and *The Slave Economy of the Old South: The Selected Essays of Ulrich Bonnell Phillips*, ed. by Eugene D. Genovese (Baton Rouge, 1968). My own appraisal of Phillips' work along with other matters may be found in Eugene D. Genovese, *In Red and Black: Marxian Explorations in Southern and Afro-American History* (New York, 1971). The outstanding alternative to Phillips' interpretation of southern slave society as a whole is Kenneth M. Stampp, *The Peculiar Institution* (New York, 1956).

Consideration of the slave revolts in the United States must begin with Herbert Aptheker, *American Negro Slave Revolts* (New York, 1943), widely criticized for exaggerations but nonetheless invaluable. In addition see Aptheker's ground-breaking essays in *To Be Free: Studies in American Negro History* (New York, 1948). See also his "Additional Data on American Maroons," *Journal of Negro History*, XXXII (October, 1947), 452–60. For other useful general accounts see Joseph C. Carroll, *Slave Insurrections in the United States* (Boston, 1938); Harvey Wish, "Slave Insurrections

Before 1861," *Journal of Negro History*, XXII (July, 1937), 299–320; Harvey Wish, "The Slave Insurrection Panic of 1856," *Journal of Southern History*, V (February–November, 1938), 206–22; and Richard Maxwell Brown, *Strain of Violence: Historical Studies of American Violence and Vigilantism* (New York, 1975), Chap. 7.

For a stimulating popular account of the revolts in the United States see Nicholas Halasz, *The Rattling Chains* (New York, 1966), esp. Chap. 5 on the effects of the Haitian Revolution. Clement Eaton, *The Freedom-of-Thought Struggle in the Old South* (Durham, N.C., 1940), is especially good on "The Fear of Servile Insurrection" (Chap. 4). A number of recent books on slave life contain thoughtful assessments of the revolts from different points of view: John W. Blassingame, *The Slave Community* (New York, 1972); Nathan Huggins, *Black Odyssey: The Afro-American Ordeal in Slavery* (New York, 1977); Leslie Howard Owens, *"This Species of Property": Slave Life and Culture in the Old South* (New York, 1976); George P. Rawick, *From Sundown to Sunup: The Making of the Black Community* (Westport, Conn., 1972); and John Anthony Scott, *Hard Trials on My Way: Slavery and the Struggle Against It, 1800–1860* (New York, 1974). For a provocative interpretation that accepts the thesis of docility see Stanley M. Elkins, *Slavery: A Problem in American Institutional and Intellectual Life* (Chicago, 1959); but also Ann J. Lane, ed., *The Debate Over Slavery: The Elkins Thesis and Its Critics* (Urbana, Ill., 1971). Of exceptional importance is the searching essay of Marion Kilson, "Towards Freedom: An Analysis of Slave Revolts in the United States," *Phylon*, XXV (Summer, 1964), 175–87, which attempts, with a good measure of success, to classify different types of revolt.

For the colonial period in general see Winthrop D. Jordan, *White Over Black: American Attitudes Toward the Negro, 1550 – 1812* (Chapel Hill, N.C., 1968). For the revolt in New York City in 1712 see Kenneth Scott, "The Slave Insurrection in New York in 1712," *New York Historical Society Quarterly*, XLV (January, 1961), 43–74. The revolt of 1712 and the conspiracy trial of 1741 are discussed in Edgar J. McManus, *Negro Slavery in New York* (Syracuse, 1966). The contemporary account of Daniel Horsmanden, *The New York Conspiracy or a History of the Negro Plot with the Journal Proceedings against the Conspirators at New York in the Years 1741–1742* (New York, 1810; 1972), makes fascinating reading about the terror struck into the white population. See also Ferenc M. Szasz, "The New York Slave Revolt of 1741: A Re-Examination," *New York History*, XXVIII (July, 1967), 215–30.

For the plots and revolts in colonial Louisiana, including the complex conspiracy at Pointe Coupée see the forthcoming book by James Thomas McGowan, or his doctoral dissertation, "Creation of a Slave Society: Louisiana Plantations in the Eighteenth Century" (University of Rochester, 1976), which brilliantly analyzes slave resistance, Indian wars, and French and Spanish politics and economics. See also Jack D. L. Holmes, "The Abortive Slave Revolt at Pointe Coupée, Louisiana, 1795," *Louisiana History*, XI (Fall, 1970), 341–62, and Tommy R. Young II, "The United States Army and the Institution of Slavery in Louisiana, 1803–1815," *Louisiana Studies*, XIII (Fall, 1974), 201–22, which sheds new light on the revolt of 1811; and James H. Dorman, "The Persistent Spectre: Slave Rebellion in Territorial Louisiana," *Louisiana History* XVIII (Fall, 1977), 389–404.

The studies of slavery in the states have materials and

analyses of the slave revolts and discussions of white fears in the absence of actual revolt. See Charles S. Sydnor, *Slavery in Mississippi* (Gloucester, Mass., 1965); Joe Gray Taylor, *Negro Slavery in Louisiana* (Baton Rouge, 1963); James Benson Sellers, *Slavery in Alabama* (University of Alabama, 1964); Charles S. Davis, *The Cotton Kingdom in Alabama* (Montgomery, 1939); Robert McColley, *Slavery and Jeffersonian Virginia* (Champaign, Ill., 1964); Jeffrey R. Brackett, *The Negro in Maryland: A Study of the Institution of Slavery* (Baltimore, 1889); Ralph Betts Flanders, *Plantation Slavery in Georgia* (Chapel Hill, N.C., 1933); John D. Milligan, "Slave Rebelliousness and the Florida Maroons," *Prologue*, VI (Spring, 1974), 4–18, is especially valuable. Orville W. Taylor, *Negro Slavery in Arkansas* (Durham, N.C., 1958); Chase C. Mooney, *Slavery in Tennessee* (Bloomington, Ind., 1957); Caleb Perry Patterson, *The Negro in Tennessee, 1790–1860* (Austin, 1922); Ivan E. McDougle, *Slavery in Kentucky, 1792–1865* (Lancaster, Pa., 1918); John Winston Coleman, *Slavery Times in Kentucky* (Chapel Hill, N.C., 1940); Howell Meadoes Henry, *The Police Control of the Slave in Southern Carolina* (Emory, Va., 1914); W. K. Moore, "An Abortive Slave Uprising," *Missouri Historical Review* (January, 1958), 123–26; and David Burns McKibben, "Negro Slave Insurrections in Mississippi, 1800–1865," *Journal of Negro History*, XXXIV (January, 1949), 73–90, which suffers from a slim evidential base.

On Texas see Alwyn Barr, *Black Texans: A History of Negroes in Texas, 1528–1971* (Austin, 1973); and Wendell G. Addington, "Slave Insurrections in Texas," *Journal of Negro History*, XXXV (October, 1950), 408–34. Also, Harold Schoen, "The Free Negro in the Republic of Texas," *South-*

western Historical Quarterly, XL (January, 1937), 169–99; William W. White, "The Texas Slave Insurrection of 1860," *Southwestern Historical Quarterly*, LII (January, 1949), 259–85; and for a skeptical reassessment, Wesley Norton, "Civil Disturbances in North Texas in 1859 and 1860," *Southwestern Historical Quarterly*, LXVIII (January, 1965), 317–41.

On the relationship of blacks and Indians and on frontier conditions generally see especially Kenneth Wiggins Porter's remarkable volume of studies, *The Negro on the Frontier* (New York, 1971), which contains the best account of the Seminole War. Also, Annie Abel, *The Slaveholding Indians* (3 vols.; Cleveland, 1915–1925); Mary Elizabeth Young, *Redskins, Ruffleshirts, and Rednecks: Indian Allotments in Alabama and Mississippi, 1830–1860* (Norman, Okla., 1960); Gary B. Nash, *Red, White, and Black* (Englewood Cliffs, N.J., 1974); Richard Maxwell Brown, *South Carolina Regulators* (Cambridge, Mass., 1963); Rembert W. Patrick, *Florida Fiasco: Rampant Rebels on the Georgia-Florida Border, 1810–1815* (Athens, Ga., 1954); David M. Potter, "The Rise of the Plantation System in Georgia," *Georgia Historical Quarterly*, XVI (June, 1932), 114–35; William S. Willis, "Divide and Rule: Red, White, and Black in the Southeast," *Journal of Negro History*, XLVIII (July, 1963), 157–76; and Willis, "Anthropology and Negroes on the Southern Colonial Frontier," in James C. Curtis and Lewis L. Gould, eds., *The Black Experience in America* (Austin, Texas, 1970); Richard K. Murdoch, "The Return of Runaway Slaves, 1790–1794," *Florida Historical Quarterly*, XXXVIII (October, 1959), 96–113; Wyatt F. Jeltz, "The Relations of Negroes and Choctaw and Chickasaw Indians," *Journal of Negro History*, XXXIII (January, 1948), 24–37; Edward Everett

Dale, "The Cherokees in the Confederacy," *Journal of Southern History*, XIII (May, 1947), 159–85.

The best study of the Stono Rebellion will be found in Peter Wood, *Black Majority* (New York, N.Y., 1974), but for the political context see also Eugene M. Sirmans, *Colonial South Carolina: A Political History, 1663–1673* (Chapel Hill, N.C., 1966). Gerald W. Mullin's chapter on Gabriel's revolt supersedes other accounts: *Flight and Rebellion: Slave Resistance in Eighteenth-Century Virginia* (New York, 1972). The discussion of slave revolt in James Hugo Johnston, *Race Relations in Virginia and Miscegenation in the South* (Amherst, Mass., 1970), is generally useful, and the account of the conspiracy of 1802 especially so.

The fullest study of the Denmark Vesey conspiracy is that of John Lofton, *Insurrection in South Carolina: The Turbulent World of Denmark Vesey* (Yellow Springs, Ohio, 1964), but see also the penetrating analysis in William W. Freehling, *Prelude to Civil War* (New York, 1966). Richard Wade minimizes the conspiracy in "The Vesey Plot: A Reconsideration," *Journal of Southern History*, XXX (May, 1964), 143–61. Freehling has adequately refuted Wade's thesis, as has Sterling Stuckey, "Remembering Denmark Vesey," *Negro Digest*, XV (February, 1966), 28–41. Important documents are available in *The Trial of Denmark Vesey*, ed. John O. Killens (Boston, 1970) and (no editor), *An Account of the Late Intended Insurrection Among a Portion of the Blacks of This City* (Charleston, 1822). The latter was reprinted in 1970 (Westport, Conn.) in a volume entitled *Slave Insurrections: Selected Documents*, which also includes Thomas Pinckney, *Reflections Occasioned by the Late Disturbance in Charleston* and Joshua Coffin, *An Account of Some of the Principal Slave Insurrections*.

See also Robert Starobin, ed., *Denmark Vesey: The Slave Conspiracy of 1822* (Englewood Cliffs, N.J., 1970) and his "Denmark Vesey's Slave Conspiracy of 1822: A Study of Rebellion and Repression," in John Bracey, *et al.*, eds., *American Slavery: The Question of Resistance* (Belmont, Calif., 1971), 142–57.

Stephen B. Oates, *The Fires of Jubilee: Nat Turner's Fierce Rebellion* (New York, 1975), combines sound scholarship and literary talent. Eric Foner's introduction to *Nat Turner* (Englewood Cliffs, N.J.), a collection of source materials, is excellent. The old study by William S. Drewry, *The Southampton Insurrection* (Washington, D.C., 1900), retains some value but is badly marred by errors and bias. F. Roy Johnson, *The Nat Turner Slave Insurrection* (Murfreesboro, 1966), is especially interesting for its discussion of religion. Herbert Aptheker's *Nat Turner's Slave Rebellion* (New York, 1966) is not as good as the chapter in his *American Negro Slave Revolts*. On the wider context see John W. Cromwell, "The Aftermath of Nat Turner's Insurrection," *Journal of Negro History*, V (April, 1920), 208–34. Of special importance is the excellent collection of documents with a generally able but sometimes cranky introduction by Henry Tragle, *The Southampton Slave Revolt of 1831* (Amherst, Mass., 1971).

For slave revolts in the North see Edgar J. McManus, *Black Bondage in the North* (Syracuse, 1973), and Arthur Zilversmit, *The First Emancipation: The Abolition of Slavery in the North* (Chicago, 1967). For a moving account of an important if unusual action see Jonathan Katz, *Resistance at Christiana* (New York, 1974), which sheds light on black resistance to the implementation of the Fugitive Slave Law.

For a good survey of black abolitionists, their attitude toward slave revolts, and their role in shaping the ideology of black America, see Benjamin Quarles, *Black Abolitionists* (New York, 1969). Also valuable is Jane H. Pease and William H. Pease, *They Who Would Be Free: Blacks' Search for Freedom, 1830–1861* (New York, 1974), which has especially interesting material on the impact of the European revolutions of 1830 and 1848 on black consciousness in the United States; and Carleton Mabee, *Black Freedom: The Nonviolent Abolitionists from 1830 Through the Civil War* (London, 1970), which has useful material on abolitionist attitudes toward slave revolt. Indispensable for the impact of the ideology of the Age of Revolution on militant blacks is Sterling Stuckey, ed., *The Ideological Origins of Black Nationalism* (Boston, 1972), for which Stuckey has written a brilliant introduction. Stanley Feldstein, *Once a Slave: The Slaves' View of Slavery* (New York, 1971) is especially good on the slaves' view of the Declaration of Independence. On the general relationship of black thought to "the complete fabric of American life," see Leroi Jones, "The Myth of 'Negro Literature,'" in Charles T. Davis and Daniel Walden, eds., *On Being Black: Writings by Afro-Americans from Frederick Douglass to the Present* (Greenwood, Conn., 1970). Among the many fine documentaries of black writings and speeches see especially Carter G. Woodson, ed., *The Mind of the Negro as Reflected in Letters Written During the Crisis, 1800–1860* (Washington, D.C., 1926); and Dorothy Porter, ed., *Early Negro Writing, 1760–1837* (Boston, 1971). On black hopes for an Afro-Saxon empire in the Caribbean see Howard H. Bell, ed., *Black Separatism and the Caribbean, 1860* (Ann Arbor, Mich., 1970).

The importance of religion to resistance, rebellion, and

accommodation has become increasingly clear, and some excellent work has recently appeared on black religion. See especially Lawrence W. Levine, *Black Culture and Black Consciousness: Afro-American Folk Thought from Slavery to Freedom* (New York, 1977). For a comprehensive analysis of the literature see Olli Alho, *The Religion of the Slaves: A Study of the Religious Tradition and Behavior of Plantation Slaves in the United States* (Helsinki, 1976). Mecham Sobel's study of the black Baptists under slavery, *Trabelin' On* (Westport, Conn., 1979), is based on fresh sources. Among the different interpretations of religious radicalism see especially Vincent Harding, "Religion and Resistance Among Antebellum American Negroes, 1800–1860," in August Meier and Elliott Rudwick, eds., *The Making of Black America* (2 vols.; New York, 1969), 179–97; Gayraud S. Wilmore, *Black Religion and Black Radicalism* (New York, 1972); and two books by Henry H. Mitchell, *Black Preaching* (Philadelphia, 1970) and *Black Belief: Folk Beliefs of Blacks in America and West Africa* (New York, 1975). My own views may be found in *Roll, Jordan, Roll: The World the Slaves Made* (New York, 1974).

The relationship between slave revolt and the abolition of the slave trade is discussed by W. E. B. Du Bois, *The Suppression of the African Slave Trade to the United States of America* (New York, 1896), which contains many insights into the impact of the Afro-Americans on world politics. The complexities of the slave trade in relation to revolt and abolition are explored further in Converse D. Clowse, *Economic Beginnings in Colonial South Carolina, 1670–1730* (Columbia, S.C., 1971); Darold D. Wax, "Georgia and the Negro Before the American Revolution," *Georgia Historical Quarterly*, LI

(March, 1967), 63–77, and "Negro Resistance to the Early American Slave Trade," *Journal of Negro History*, LI (January, 1966), 1–15; Lorenzo J. Greene, "Mutiny on the Slave Ships," *Phylon*, V (Fourth Quarter, 1944), 346–54; James Pope-Hennesy, *Sins of the Fathers* (New York, 1966); Document, "A Slave Mutiny, 1764," *Connecticut Historical Society Bulletin*, XXXI (January, 1966), 30–32; Johannes Postma, "Slaving Techniques and Treatment of Slaves: The Dutch Activities on the Guinea Coast," in Stanley L. Engerman and Eugene D. Genovese, eds., *Race and Slavery in the Western Hemisphere: Quantitative Studies* (Princeton, N.J., 1973), 33–50; Patrick S. Brady, "The Slave Trade and Sectionalism in South Carolina, 1787–1808," *Journal of Southern History*, XXXVIII (November, 1972), 601–20; Howard Jones, "The Peculiar Institution and National Honor: The Case of the Creole Slave Revolt," *Civil War History*, XXI (March, 1975), 28–50. For the domestic slave trade in general and black resistance to it see Frederic Bancroft, *Slave-Trading in the Old South* (Baltimore, 1931).

Brazilian slave revolts and *quilombos* are surveyed in Clóvis Moura, *Rebeliões da senzala: quilombos, insurreicões, guerrilhas* (São Paulo, 1959), and are related to wider black struggles in Luiz Luna, *O negro na luta contra a escravidão* (Rio de Janeiro, 1968). Also useful is José Alípio Goulart, *Da fuga ao suicídio* (Rio de Janeiro, 1972). Aderbal Jurema, *Insurreicões negras no Brasil* (Recife, 1935), presents a stimulating if schematic early Marxist interpretation. Carl Degler has a different interpretation in *Neither Black nor White* (New York, 1971). Revolts and *quilombos* are assessed, often with valuable insight, in Raimondo Nina Rodrigues, *Os africanos no Brasil* (São Paulo, 1932); Arthur Ramos, *The Negro in Brazil*

(Washington, D.C., 1939); and Edison Carneiro, *Ladinos e crioulos: estudos sôbre o negro no Brasil* (Rio de Janeiro, 1964). Especially interesting despite many arguable formulations is the treatment of the religious dimension in Roger Bastide, *Les religions africaines au Brésil* (Paris, 1960). On guerrilla bases see Stuart B. Schwartz, "The Mocambo: Slave Resistance in Colonial Bahia," *Journal of Social History*, III (Summer, 1970), 313–33. See also, Schwartz, "Resistance and Accommodation in Eighteenth-Century Brazil: The Slaves' View of Slavery," *Hispanic American Historical Review*, LVII (February, 1977), 69–81; and Cleveland Donald, Jr., "Slave Resistance and Abolitionism in Brazil: The Campista Case, 1879–1888," *Luso-Brazilian Review*, XIII (1976), 182–93. For the role of women in Brazil and Spanish America see Ann Pescatello, *Power and Pawn* (Westport, Conn., 1976).

For the wider context of black action see especially the works of C. R. Boxer: *The Dutch in Brazil* (Oxford, 1957); *Salvador de Sá and the Struggle for Brazil and Angola* (London, 1952); and *The Golden Age of Brazil* (Berkeley, Calif., 1962). The works of Gilberto Freyre remain arresting, although his interpretations of revolts and *quilombos* range from doubtful to preposterous in their special pleading. See especially *The Masters and the Slaves* (New York, 1956) and *The Mansions and the Shanties* (New York, 1963). The admirable books of Caio Prado Junior devote attention to black history: *The Colonial Background of Modern Brazil* (Berkeley, Calif., 1967); *História econômica do Brasil* (7th ed.; São Paulo, 1962); and *Evolução política do Brasil e outros estudos* (4th ed.; São Paulo, 1963). For the early period see Pedro Calmon, *História social do Brasil* (3 vols.; São Paulo, 1937–1939); and for the wider struggles of the eighteenth century see Kenneth R. Maxwell, *Conflicts and Conspiracies: Brazil and Portugal, 1750–1808* (Cambridge, 1973). For the mining region see the valuable study by Waldemar de Almeida Barbosa, *Negros e quilombos em Minas Gerais* (Belo Horizonte, 1972).

The debate over the role of blacks, free and slave, during the abolition crisis of the second half of the nineteenth century continues apace. Of special importance is Emilia Viotti da Costa, *Da senzala à colonia* (São Paulo, 1966). Among the works in English that directly treat the issue of violence and abolitionist activity in relation to political and economic developments, the most satisfactory is Robert B. Toplin, *The Abolition of Slavery in Brazil* (New York, 1972). See also his article, "Upheaval, Violence, and the Abolition of Slavery in Brazil: The Case of São Paulo," *Hispanic American Historical Review*, XLIX (November, 1969), 639–55. But for other viewpoints see Peter Eisenberg, *The Sugar Industry in Pernambuco, 1840–1910: Modernization Without Change* (Berkeley, 1974), and Robert Conrad, *The Destruction of Brazilian Slavery, 1850–1888* (Berkeley, 1972).

Many of the works already cited discuss Palmares and the Bahia revolts, but several special studies are essential. On Palmares see especially Edison Carneiro, *O quilombo dos Palmares* (São Paulo, 1947), with some valuable documents. Of the several journal articles see especially R. K. Kent, "An African State in Brazil," *Journal of African History*, VI, no. 2 (1965), 161–75; and Ernesto Ennes, "The Palmares 'Republic' of Pernambuco: Its Final Destruction, 1697," *Americas*, V (October, 1948), 200–216. Ennes has edited a volume of documents: *As guerras nos Palmares* (São Paulo, 1938). A few of these have been translated into English; see Richard Morse, ed., *The Bandeirantes* (New York, 1965), 115–26.

The revolts in Bahia from 1807 to 1835 have been critically surveyed by Howard Prince, "Slave Rebellion in Bahia, 1807–1835" (Ph.D. dissertation, Columbia University, 1972); and João José Reis, "Black Revolts in Bahia, 1807–1835" (M.A. thesis, University of Minnesota, 1978), which provides an excellent evaluation from a Marxist viewpoint. See also Reis, "A Elite Baiana Face os Movimentos Sociais, Bahia: 1824–1840," *Revista de História* (São Paulo), *CVIII* (1976), 341–84.

The old two-part account by Abbé Ignace Etienne, although marred by extreme bias and factual errors, still tells a good story: "La secte musulmane des Malès du Brésil et leur révolte en 1835," *Anthropos*, IV (1909), 99–105, 405–15. Contacts between Bahia and Africa are discussed in Pierre Verger, *Flux et reflux de la traite des Nègres entre le Golfe de Benin et Bahia de Todos os Santos* (Paris, 1968); and José Honorio Rodrigues, *Brazil and Africa* (Berkeley, 1965), which, however, certainly overestimates the role of the Hausa. For a challenging interpretation by a tough-minded anti-Marxist scholar see R. K. Kent, "African Revolt in Bahia: 24–25 January 1935," *Journal of Social History*, III (Summer, 1970), 334–56.

For the background of African Islam see especially J. Spencer Trimingham, *Islam in West Africa* (Oxford, 1959), and *A History of Islam in West Africa* (London, 1962); M. G. Smith, "Slavery and Emancipation in Two Societies," *Social and Economic Studies*, II (December, 1954), 239–90; C. Daryll Forde, *The Yoruba-Speaking Peoples of Southwestern Nigeria* (London, 1962); and Allan G. B. Fisher and Humphrey J. Fisher, *Slavery and Muslim Society in Africa* (Garden City, N.Y., 1971). For the relevant features of the classical

Muslim political tradition see especially Reuben Levy, *The Social Structure of Islam* (Cambridge, 1957); Erwin I. J. Rosenthal, *Political Thought in Medieval Islam* (Cambridge, 1962); and the theoretically rich if somewhat contentious Marxist analyses of Maxime Rodinson: *Mohammed* (New York, 1971) and *Islam and Capitalism* (New York, 1973).

For Spanish America see the excellent chapter on slave revolt and resistance in Leslie B. Rout, Jr., *The African Experience in Spanish America* (Cambridge, 1976). For a general discussion, especially useful for Peru, see Rolando Mellafe, *La esclavitud en Hispanoamérica* (Buenos Aires, 1964). For another, especially useful for Santo Domingo, see Ralph H. Vigil, "Negro Slaves and Rebels in The Spanish Possessions, 1503–1558," *Historian*, XXXIII (1971), 637–55. Among the many admirable features of John Lynch, *The Spanish American Revolutions, 1808–1826* (New York, 1973), is the attention paid to black participation and autonomous action.

Sixteenth-century revolts and maroon warfare are surveyed in Carlos Federico Guillot, *Negros rebeldes y negros cimarrones: perfil afroaméricano en la historia del Nuevo Mundo durante el siglo XVI* (Montevideo, 1961). There are several useful studies of black revolt in Mexico: David M. Davidson, "Negro Slave Control and Resistance to Spanish Rule in Colonial Mexico," *Journal of Negro History*, LII (April, 1967), 89–103; Gonzalo Aguirre Beltrán, *Cuijla: esbozo etnográfico de un pueblo negro* (Mexico, 1958); and Octaviano Corro R., *Los cimarrones en Vera Cruz y el Fundación de Amapa* (n.p., 1951). Valuable for Mexican-American tensions over slave defections from Texas is Ronnie C. Tyler, "Fugitive Slaves in Mexico," *Journal of Negro History*, LVII (January, 1972),

1–12. For a valuable general work see Colin A. Palmer, *Slaves of the White God* (Cambridge, Mass., 1976). For the role of blacks and Indians in the complex struggle for Central America, see Troy S. Floyd's spirited and well-written *The Anglo-Spanish Struggle for Mosquitia* (Albuquerque, N.M., 1967). Also, Luís A. Diez Castillo, *Los cimarrones y el esclavitud en Panamá* (Panama, 1968).

On Venezuela see Miguel Acosta Saignes, *Vida de los esclavos en Venezuela* (Caracas, 1967); and Federico Brito Figueroa, *Las insurrecciones de los esclavos negros en las sociedad colonial venezolana* (Caracas, 1961), which also has an important preface by Rodolfo Quintero, "El nuevo sentido de la historia venezolana." On the revolt of 1730 see Carlos Felice Cardot, *La rebelión de Andresote: Valles del Yaracuy, 1730–1733* (2nd ed.; Bogota, 1957); on the revolt of 1749 see Héctor Garciá Chuecos, "Una insurrección de negros en los días de la colonia," *Revista de Historia de América*, No. 29 (June, 1959); on Coro see Pedro Manuel Arcaya, *Insurrección de los negros de la Serranía de Coro* (Caracas, 1949).

For Columbia generally see the excellent study by Jaime Jaramillo Uribe, "Esclavos y señores en la sociedad colombiana del siglo XVIII," *Anuario Colombiano de Historia Social y de la Cultura*, I (1963), 3–62. For the relationship of black religion to slave resistance and subsequent black struggles, see Michael Taussig, "Black Religion and Resistance in Colombia: Three Centuries of Social Struggle in the Cauca Valley," *Marxist Perspectives*, II, 6 (Summer, 1979). Among the studies of the *palenques* and related subjects see especially Aquiles Escalante, "Notas sobre el palenque de San Basilio, una comunidad negra en Colombia," *Divulgaciones Etno-*

lógicas, III (1954), 207–59; Derek Bickerton and Escalante examine language and culture in "Palenquero: A Spanish-Based Creole of Northern Colombia," *Lingua*, XXIV (February, 1970), 254–67. See also Robert C. West, *Colonial Placer Mining in Colombia* (Baton Rouge, 1952); and David Pavy, "The Provenience of Colombian Negroes," *Journal of Negro History*, LII (January, 1967), 35–58.

Black resistance in Paraguay was largely nonrevolutionary for reasons discussed in Josefina Plá, *Hermano negro: la esclavitud en Paraguay* (Madrid, 1972). On Peru see especially Frederick P. Bowser's fine book, *The African Slave in Colonial Peru, 1524–1650* (Stanford, 1974). And there is a good discussion of black resistance within the special conditions of Puerto Rico in Luís M. Diaz Soler, *Historia de la esclavitud negra en Puerto Rico, 1493–1890* (Madrid, 1953). See also, Guillermo A. Baralt, "Conclusiones breves de conspiraciones, sublevaciones y revueltas de esclavos en Puerto Rico," *Sixth Annual Conference of Caribbean Historians* (Puerto Rico, 1975).

The revolts in Cuba, even more readily than elsewhere, must be studied in relation to more general liberal and national movements. See especially Francisco Pérez de la Riva, *La habitación rural en cuba* (Havana, 1952). Also, Fernando Ortiz, *Hampa afro-cubana: los negros esclavos* (Havana, 1916); H. H. S. Aimes, *A History of Slavery in Cuba, 1511 to 1868* (New York, 1907); Herbert Klein, *Slavery in the Americas* (Chicago, 1967); Franklin W. Knight, *Slave Society in Cuba During the Nineteenth Century* (Madison, Wisc., 1970); Arthur F. Corwin, *Spain and the Abolition of Slavery in Cuba, 1817–1886* (Austin, Texas, 1967); and Philip Foner, *A History of Cuba and Its Relations with the United States* (2 vols.;

New York, 1962). Valuable for the social setting of early struggles is Kenneth F. Kiple, *Blacks in Colonial Cuba, 1774–1899* (Gainesville, Fla., 1976). Among the studies of slavery that shed particular light on the development of resistance movements are: Roland T. Ely, *Cuando reinaba su majestad el azúcar* (Buenos Aires, 1963); Raúl Cepero Bonilla, *Obras históricas* (Havana, 1963); and especially Manuel Moreno Fraginals, *The Sugarmill* (New York, 1976). Cuba and Saint-Domingue are compared in Gwendolyn Midlo Hall, *Social Control in Slave Plantation Societies: A Comparison of St.-Domingue and Cuba* (Baltimore, 1971). For a fascinating account by a runaway slave see Esteban Montejo, *The Autobiography of a Runaway Slave* (New York, 1968).

For particularly acute analyses of black struggles in Cuba and elsewhere see the work of José Luciano Franco: *Afroamérica* (Havana, 1961); "Cuatros siglos de la lucha por la libertad; los palenques," *Revista de la Biblioteca Nacional José Martí*, IX (January–March, 1967), 5–44; *La conspiración de Aponte* (Havana, 1963); "La conspiración de Morales," *Revista de la Universidad de Oriente*, VI (March, 1972), 128–33; *Plácido: una polemica que tiene cien años y otros ensayos* (Havana, 1964); *Revoluciones y conflictos internationales en el Caribe, 1789–1854* (Havana, 1965), Vol. II of *La batalla por el dominio del Caribe y el Golfo de México* (3 vols.; Havana, 1964–1966).

See also Margarita Dalton, "Los depósitos de los cimarrones en el siglo XIX," *Etnología y Folklore*, III (1967), 5–29; José de Jesus Marquez, "Conspiración de Aponte," *Revista Cubana*, XIX (1894), 441–54, and *Plácido y los conspiradores de 1844* (Havana, 1894); Pedro Deschamps Chapeaux, "Cimarrones urbanos," *Revista de la Biblioteca Nacional José*

Martí, XI (May–August, 1969), 145–64; Francisco González del Valle, *La conspiración de la Escalera* (Havana, 1925); Clément Lanier, "Cuba et la conspiration d'Apunte en 1812," *Revue Société Haitienne d'Histoire, de Geographie et de Geologie*, XXIII (July, 1952), 19–30; Fernando Ortiz, "Las rebeliones de los afro-cubanos," *Revista Bimestre Cubana*, IV (March–April, 1910), 97–112; Francisco Pérez de la Riva, "El negro y la tierra, el conuco y el palenque," *Revista Bimestre Cubana*, LVIII (September–December, 1946), 97–139; Cirilo Villaverde, *Palenque de negros cimarrones* (San Antonio de los Banos, 1890). An excellent study is Vidal Morales y Morales, *Iniciadores y primer mártires de la revolución cubana* (3 vols.; Havana, 1931); very good is Elias Entralgo, *La liberación étnica cubana* (Havana, 1955); and valuable material with conservative interpretation may be found in Justo P. Zaragoza, *Las insurrecciones en Cuba* (2 vols.; Madrid, 1872–1873).

The slave revolts in the Caribbean region occurred amidst great-power rivalries and recurring warfare, as the work of José Luciano Franco especially illuminates. For this setting see such works as: Arthur Percival Newton, *The European Nations in the West Indies, 1493–1688* (London, 1933); J. H. Parry, *Trade and Dominion: The European Overseas Empires in the Eighteenth Century* (New York, 1971); James Alexander Robertson, "The English Attack on Cartagena in 1741; and Plans for an Attack on Panama," *Hispanic American Historical Review*, II (February, 1919), 62–71.

The forthcoming studies of slave revolt in the British Caribbean by Anthony Synnott and Michael Craton both promise to be outstanding. Sir Alan Burns, *History of the British West Indies* (London, 1954), contains much material on the slave revolts and offers a useful survey of regional history. Other works that help set the context for slave revolt in a theatre of war and diplomatic intrigue are: Carl and Roberta Bridenbaugh, *No Peace Beyond the Line: The English in the Caribbean, 1624–1690* (New York, 1972); and Frank Wesley Pitman, *The Development of the British West Indies, 1700–1763* (London, 1963). Two works on the slave regimes are of particular value: the older but still useful study by Lowell Joseph Ragatz, *The Fall of the Planter Class in the British Caribbean, 1763–1833* (New York, 1971; first published, 1928), and Richard S. Dunn's excellent *Sugar and Slaves: The Rise of the Planter Class in the English West Indies, 1624–1713* (Chapel Hill, N.C., 1972).

Other works that treat British slavery generally and shed light on the slave revolts are: Eric Williams, *Capitalism and Slavery* (Chapel Hill, N.C., 1944); Michael Craton, *Sinews of Empire* (Garden City, N.Y., 1974); Wesley Frank Pitman, "Slavery on the British West India Plantations in the Eighteenth Century," *Journal of Negro History*, XI (October, 1926), 584–668; Edward Braithwaite, *The Development of Creole Society in Jamaica, 1770–1820* (Oxford, 1971); Michael Craton and James Walvin, *A Jamaican Plantation: The History of Worthy Park, 1670–1970* (Toronto, 1970); Michael Craton, *Searching for the Invisible Man: Slaves and Plantation Life in Jamaica* (Cambridge, Mass., 1978). The ethnic factor in the revolts is suggestively explored by Monica Schuler in two articles: "The Ethnic Slave Rebellions in the Caribbean and the Guianas," *Journal of Social History*, III (Summer, 1970), 374–85, and "Akan Slave Rebellions in the British Caribbean," *Savacou*, I (1970), 8–31.

Orlando Patterson, *The Sociology of Slavery* (London,

1967), among other virtues, contains a thoughtful analysis of the slave revolts. Philip Curtin, *Two Jamaicas* (Cambridge, Mass., 1955), adds many insights into the international context. B. W. Higman, *Slave Population and Economy in Jamaica, 1807–1834* (Cambridge, 1834), is excellent for the economic context. The great revolt of 1831 has been well studied by Mary Reckord (Turner), "The Jamaican Slave Rebellion of 1831," *Past & Present*, No. 40 (July, 1968), 108–25. Two older works remain valuable: Bryan Edwards, *The History, Civil and Commercial, of the British West Indies* (5 vols.; London; several editions); and Edward Long, *The History of Jamaica* (London, 1774).

The standard work on the maroon wars is R. C. Dallas, *The History of the Maroons, from their Origin to the Establishment of their Chief Tribe at Sierra Leone* (2 vols.; London, 1803). See also the analysis of Orlando Patterson, marred primarily by a biased and unconvincing assessment of Cudjoe: "Slavery and Slave Revolts: A Socio-Historical Analysis of the First Maroon War, 1655–1740," *Social and Economic Studies*, XIX (September, 1970), 289–325. Robin Winks, *The Blacks in Canada* (New Haven, Conn., 1971) takes the Jamaican maroons through Nova Scotia; and Christopher Fyfe, *A History of Sierra Leone* (London, 1962), picks them up thereafter. Essential for an understanding of the maroons is Barbara Kopytoff's brilliant and path-breaking new work: See especially, "Jamaican Maroon Political Organization: The Effects of the Treaties," *Social and Economic Studies*, XXV (June, 1976), 87–105; also, "The Early Political Development of Jamaican Maroon Societies," *William & Mary Quarterly*, XXXV (April, 1978), 287–307; and "The Development of

160

Jamaican Maroon Ethnicity," *Caribbean Quarterly*, XXII (June–September, 1976), 33–50.

The role of women awaits adequate attention, but for an introduction see Lucille Mathurin's lively, popular little book, *The Rebel Woman in the British West Indies During Slavery* (Kingston, 1975); and Alan Tuelon, "Nanny—Maroon Chieftainess," *Caribbean Quarterly*, XIX (December, 1973), 20–27.

For the Leeward Islands see the outstanding book by Elsa V. Goveia, *Slave Society in the British Leeward Islands at the End of the Eighteenth Century* (New Haven, 1965). For Trinidad and Tobago see Eric Williams, *History of the Peoples of Trinidäd and Tobago* (London, 1962); and V. S. Naipaul, *The Loss of El Dorado* (London, 1969). For Barbados and the revolt of 1816 see Vincent T. Harlow, *A History of Barbados* (Oxford, 1926); J. Harry Bennett, *Bondsmen and Bishops* (Berkeley, Calif., 1958); Claude Levy, "Barbados: The Last Years of Slavery, 1823–1833," *Journal of Negro History*, XLIV (October, 1959), 309–45; and Jerome S. Handler and Frederick W. Lange, *Plantation Slavery in Barbados: An Archaeological and Historical Investigation* (Cambridge, Mass., 1978).

For British Guiana there is useful material in D. A. G. Waddell's little book, *The West Indies and the Guianas* (Englewood Cliffs, N.J., 1967). But see especially J. J. Hartsinck, "The Story of the Great Rebellion in Berbice in 1762," *Journal of the British Guiana Museum and Zoo and the Royal Agricultural and Commercial Society*, Nos. 20–27 (8 parts: 1958–1960). Roy Arthur Glasgow relates the struggles of the slavery era to more recent ones in *Guyana: Race and Politics Among Africans and East Indians* (The Hague, 1970). Especially rich is Rawle Farley, "Aspects of the Economic History of British Guiana, 1781–1852: A Study of Economic and Social Change on the Southern Caribbean Frontier" (Ph.D. dissertation, University of London, 1956). I have also profited from a paper as yet unpublished, so far as I know: Robert Moore, "Slave Rebellions in Guyana" (3rd Annual Conference of Caribbean Historians; Guiana, 1971).

For the revolts and maroon communities in Surinam, Richard Price has provided an excellent bibliographic guide: *The Guiana Maroons: A Bibliographic Introduction* (Baltimore, 1976). See also his *Saramaka Social Structure: Analysis of "Bush Negro" Society* (Rio Piedras, Puerto Rico, 1973), and his own articles cited in *Guiana Maroons*. Also essential are: Silvia W. de Groot, *Djuka Society and Social Change* (Assen, 1969); R. A. J. Van Lier, *Frontier Society: A Social Analysis of the History of Surinam* (The Hague, 1971); and Morton C. Kahn, *Djuka: The Bush Negroes of Dutch Guiana* (New York, 1931), which emphasizes continuity with the African experience. Still useful are Melville J. Herskovits, *Rebel Destiny* (New York, 1934), and Melville J. and Frances Herskovits, *Suriname Folk-lore* (New York, 1936). For the larger context see C. R. Boxer, *The Dutch Seaborne Empire, 1600–1800* (London, 1965). Good reading and an invaluable source is (Captain) John Stedman, *Narrative of a Five Years' Expedition Against the Revolted Negroes of Surinam* (Amherst, Mass., 1971; first published 1796).

The two great risings in the Danish Virgin Islands are discussed in Waldemar Westergaard, *The Danish West Indies Under Company Rule* (New York, 1917). See also, John L. Anderson, *Night of the Silent Drums* (New York, 1975), on the revolt of 1733. For some interesting observations see Gordon K. Lewis, "An Introductory Note to the Study of the Virgin Islands," *Caribbean Studies*, VII (July, 1968), 5–22. For the great revolution in Saint-Domingue, in addition to the outstanding works of C. L. R. James and José Luciano Franco, see George F. Tyson, Jr., ed., *Toussaint L'Ouverture*, which provides an incisive introduction to some good readings. Among the hostile interpretations of the revolution see especially T. Lothrop Stoddard, *The French Revolution in San Domingo* (Boston, 1914), or Harold Palmer Davis, *Black Democracy* (Rev. ed.; New York, 1937). James G. Leyburn, *The Haitian People* (New Haven, 1966), combines a fine historical sketch with an outstanding interpretation of Haitian life. Of special interest is Charles Frostin, *Les révoltes blanches à Saint-Domingue aux XVIIe et XVIII siècles* (Paris, 1975). For the religious question see Odette Mennesson-Rigaud, "Le rôle de Vaudou dans l'indépendance d'Haiti," *Presence Africaine*, nos. 17–18 (February–May, 1958), 43–67; and Alfred Métraux, *Voodoo in Haiti* (New York, 1972). See also Hubert Cole, *Christophe, King of Haiti* (London, 1967); and Richard Pattee, *Jean Jacques Dessalines: Fundador de Haiti* (Havana, 1936).

For the French West Indies in general see Gaston Martin, *Histoire de l'esclavage dans les colonies françaises* (Paris, 1949). The only overview in English is Shelby T. McCloy, *The Negro in the French West Indies* (Lexington, Ky., 1966), which is disappointing. The extensive writings of Gabriel Debien are invaluable; see especially "Le marronage aux Antilles Françaises au XVIIIe siècle," *Caribbean Studies*, VI (October, 1966), 3–44; "Les esclaves marrons à Saint-Domingue en 1764,"

Jamaican Historical Review, LXI (1966), 9–20. Essential is Yvan Debbasch, "Le marronage: essai sur la désertion de l'esclave antillais," *L'Anné Sociologique* (3rd Series, 1961), 1–112, and (3rd Series, 1962), 117–95. More polemical is Jean Fouchard, *Les marrons de la liberté* (Paris, 1972). See also Roger Bastide, "Nègres marrons et nègres libres," *Annales: Economies—Sociétés—Civilisations*, XX (January–February, 1965), 169–74.

The important role of religion in the slave revolts compels some attention to the vast literature on millennialism and on the historical relationship of radical religion to revolutionary movements. Norman Cohn, *The Pursuit of the Millennium* (London, 1957), notwithstanding its fierce conservative partisanship, remains indispensable. Also cool to revolutionary movements but remarkably rich and judicious is Guenter Lewy, *Religion and Revolution* (New York, 1974). For the political implications of the prophetic tradition it is still best to begin with the work of Max Weber. See especially *The Sociology of Religion* (Boston, 1963) and *Ancient Judaism* (Glencoe, Ill., 1952). For a challenging interpretation of the radical tradition see Rosemary Radford Reuther, *The Radical Kingdom* (New York, 1970). More directly relevant is Vittorio Lanternari, *The Religions of the Oppressed* (New York, 1963); Peter Worsley, *The Trumpet Shall Sound* (London, 1956); and Ambrogio Donini, *Lineamenti di storia delle religioni* (Rome, 1964). Two little books by Eric Hobsbawm, while not directly focused on religion, make essential contributions to the social analysis of popular movements in which religion often figured: *Primitive Rebels* (Manchester, England, 1959) and *Bandits* (New York, 1969).

The psychological aspect of revolt and revolution has been getting a good deal of attention lately, with indifferent, not to say miserable, results. Of value, however, has been the work on colonialism, which bears directly on problems of racism and the dynamics of class domination. Alas, the best book is by a conservative whose sympathy for the oppressors can hardly be ignored: Octave Mannoni, *Prospero and Caliban: The Psychology of Colonization* (London, 1956). The work of Albert Memmi should be consulted: *Dominated Man* (New York, 1968) and *The Colonizer and the Colonized* (Boston, 1965). The work of Frantz Fanon will not pass muster as scientific psychology but retains great interest for its many insights and for the point of view of the colonized that it brings to bear. See especially *Black Skin, White Masks* (New York, 1967) and *The Wretched of the Earth* (New York, 1963). For a critique of these authors see Elizabeth Fox-Genovese and Eugene D. Genovese, "On the Psychology of Colonialism: A Critique of Leading Theories" (forthcoming).

Some acquaintance with the slave revolts of the ancient world will be helpful. The principal study is J. Vogt, *Zur Struktur der antiken Sklavenkriege* (Mainz, 1957); but see also M. I. Finley, *A History of Sicily: Ancient Sicily to the Arab Conquest* (New York, 1958), and *The Ancient Economy* (Berkeley, Calif., 1973). Also, P. Green, "The First Sicilian Slave War," *Past & Present*, No. 20 (1961), 10–29. Two essays by the learned Soviet historian Nikolai A. Mashkin are available in English. Valuable material with an untenable thesis will be found in "The Workers' Revolution and the Fall of the Western Roman Empire," *Journal of General Education*, V (October, 1950), 70–74. Much more compelling is his interpretation of the religious dimension: "Eschatology and Messianism in the Final Period of the Roman Republic," *Philosophy and Phenomenological Research*, X (December, 1949), 206–28.

Index

Index

Canada, 134
Cape Verde Islands, 13
Capitalism, xv–xvii, xxi–xxii, 83,
    118
Caribbean Islands: European involve-
    ment, xvi, 21–23, 33–39 *passim*,
    51, 55–68 *passim*, 83–89 *passim*,
    101–105 *passim*, 112, 121, 158–
    62; slave revolts, xxii, 2, 4, 6,
    12–28 *passim*, 33–38, 42, 58, 59,
    79, 100, 111, 112, 135, 158–60.
    See also specific countries
Caribbean Transformations (Mintz), 89
Carneiro, Edison, 61
Carter, Landon, 16
Castro, Raúl, 93
Charleston, S.C., 4, 8–10, 17, 46,
    48, 116
Cherniavsky, Michael, 25, 85
Christianity, 7, 28, 32, 45–48, 102,
    103, 130
Christophe, Henri, 86, 88, 89, 97
Cities and slave revolts, 13–14,
    31–32
Civil liberties, suppression of,
    114–17
Civil War, 41, 69, 111
Clark, Lewis, 25
Collaboration, 10–11
Colombia, 13–14, 38, 39, 58, 77,
    155–56
Cortes, Hernando, 58
Counterrevolution, 88–90, 93–94
Craft, William, 235
Creole slaves, 12, 18–20, 31–42
    passim, 54, 55, 97–102
Cuba, 12, 21, 38, 76, 95, 98, 99,
    156–58
Cudjoe, 65–66
Cumby, Green, 77

Dallas, R. C., 65–66, 80
Davis, David Brion, xxi, 87, 112
Declaration of Independence, 45, 49,

126, 133, 135, 136, 148. *See also*
    Democratic-bourgeois ideology
Degler, Carl, 40
Democratic-bourgeois ideology,
    xiii–xiv, xvii–xxii, 1–2, 92–94,
    97, 118–19, 121, 126–37, 148
Denmark, 21, 121
Deslondes, Charles, 43
Dessalines, 88, 105
Douglass, Frederick, 131–33
Drake, Sir Francis, 21
Draper, Theodore, 134
Du Bois, W. E. B., xxi, 20, 93, 95,
    113, 114, 140
Dunn, Richard, 37

Edward, Bryan, 64
Emancipation: rumors of, 24–25, 26,
    35, 36, 38; of slaves, 25–26, 37,
    97, 116, 120–21
Emancipation Proclamation, 97
England, xvi, 2, 19–38 *passim*, 42,
    55–70 *passim*, 83–88 *passim*, 93,
    101–105, 112, 135, 158–60
Ennes, Ernesto, 61
European powers: in Caribbean, xvi,
    20–23, 33–39 *passim*, 45, 51,
    55–68 *passim*, 83–89 *passim*,
    101–105 *passim*, 112, 121, 158–
    62; and maroons, 51–52, 54, 60,
    63–67. *See also* specific countries

Fanon, Frantz, 28
Ferdinand VII, 95
Florida, 21, 42, 49, 69, 72, 76, 79
Fourth of July, 126–37
France, xvi, xvii, 21, 22, 26, 39, 45,
    51, 58, 67, 68, 70, 86–89, 105,
    121
Franco, José Luciano, xxi
Free Negroes, 31–32, 43, 59–60,
    133–37. *See also* Blacks; Maroons;
    Slaves
French Revolution, xix–xx, 34, 36,

Index

Index

Index

45, 48, 68–69, 70, 116
Virgin Islands, 162–63

Wade, Richard, 14
Walker, David, 96
Wall, Bennett, 15, 76

War of Jenkins' Ear, 26
Watkins, William, 96
West Indies, 111, 163–64
Williams, Gwyn, 109
The World the Slaveholders Made
(Genovese), xv, 2n